Poems
of Love *and*
Friendship

Poems
of Love and
Friendship

ARCTURUS

ARCTURUS

This edition published in 2018 by Arcturus Publishing Limited
26/27 Bickels Yard, 151–153 Bermondsey Street,
London SE1 3HA

ISBN: 978-1-78428-854-9
DA005435UK

Printed in China

Contents

Introduction

*L*ove. It's all you need, said the Beatles. It makes the world go round, said medieval monks. It conquers all, said the poet Virgil; surrender to it.

Perhaps poets will always describe it best. Aspects of it, at least. Love wears many colours and takes many forms, inspiring poets across the centuries and across cultures.

In Regency England, Lord Byron captured the impact of love at first sight. The morning after the night before, he wrote:

"She walks in beauty, like the night

Of cloudless climes and starry skies"

William Blake, a radical who rejected the conventional, respectable ideas of the eighteenth century, captured the misery of unrequited love. 'Love's Secret' is a poem by a man who proposed and was turned down.

By contrast, Anne Bradstreet was born to a wealthy Puritan family in Northampton, England and emigrated to America in 1630. Her poem 'To My Dear and Loving Husband' pays testimony to the depths of her love for him but can also be read in terms of her faith: love here on earth offers its own form of salvation.

There is another love, too – the love of parents for their children. 'Golden Slumbers' is a lullaby written during the reign of Elizabeth I, famous today after it was sung by Paul McCartney on the album 'Abbey Road'.

Read 'Mother to Child' by Charlotte Perkins Gilman and remember that it was written by a woman who had experienced severe depression after the birth of her daughter in 1885. So severe, in fact, that Perkins Gilman became suicidal and even suggested divorce as the only way to ensure her daughter's safety.

Children have inspired many of the most familiar poems in this collection. Travel with 'The Owl and the Pussy-Cat' or fight the 'Jabberwocky' – thanks to their authors, Edward Lear and Lewis Carroll, who themselves never had children. And enjoy 'The Night Before Christmas', first recited by Clement Clarke Moore to his family in his New York home on Christmas Eve, 1822.

In New York a century later, Hart Crane wrote a long poem 'The Bridge', which begins with his ode 'To Brooklyn Bridge', consciously echoing the romantic traditions of earlier poets. In 1802, William Wordsworth had described the beauty of London and the Thames in 'Composed Upon Westminster Bridge', and the same subject matter would also inspire Oscar Wilde's 'Symphony in Yellow'.

Sometimes, though, a poet must be far away to remember what he loves. In 1798, Wordsworth was living in Germany and acutely homesick, which later inspired his poem 'I Travelled Among Unknown Men'. In 1845, Robert Browning was travelling in Italy when he found himself wishing to be in England "Now that April's there".

Such longing is familiar to us all. In describing their own experiences, poets give us emotions we can all recognise. Their words describe our own lives, our own dreams, and our own loves.

Family and Home

A Cradle Song

Sweet dreams, form a shade
O'er my lovely infant's head!
Sweet dreams of pleasant streams
By happy, silent, moony beams!

Sweet Sleep, with soft down
Weave thy brows an infant crown!
Sweet Sleep, angel mild,
Hover o'er my happy child!

Sweet smiles, in the night
Hover over my delight!
Sweet smiles, mother's smiles,
All the livelong night beguiles.

Sweet moans, dovelike sighs,
Chase not slumber from thy eyes!
Sweet moans, sweeter smiles,
All the dovelike moans beguiles.

Sleep, sleep, happy child!
All creation slept and smiled.
Sleep, sleep, happy sleep,
While o'er thee thy mother weep.

Sweet babe, in thy face
Holy image I can trace;
Sweet babe, once like thee
Thy Maker lay, and wept for me:

Wept for me, for thee, for all,
When He was an infant small.
Thou His image ever see,
Heavenly face that smiles on thee!

Smiles on thee, on me, on all,
Who became an infant small;
Infant smiles are His own smiles;
Heaven and earth to peace beguiles.

William Blake

Mother And Babe

I see the sleeping babe, nestling the breast of its mother;
The sleeping mother and babe — hush'd, I study them long
and long.

Walt Whitman

Cradle Song

Golden slumbers kiss your eyes,
Smiles awake you when you rise;
Sleep, pretty wantons, do not cry,
And I will sing a lullaby,
Rock them, rock them, lullaby.

Care is heavy, therefore sleep you,
You are care, and care must keep you;
Sleep, pretty wantons, do not cry,
And I will sing a lullaby,
Rock them, rock them, lullaby.

Thomas Dekker

A Child's Laughter

All the bells of heaven may ring,
All the birds of heaven may sing,
All the wells on earth may spring,
All the winds on earth may bring
All sweet sounds together;
Sweeter far than all things heard,
Hand of harper, tone of bird,
Sound of woods at sundawn stirred,
Welling water's winsome word,
Wind in warm wan weather,

One thing yet there is, that none
Hearing ere its chime be done
Knows not well the sweetest one
Heard of man beneath the sun,
Hoped in heaven hereafter;
Soft and strong and loud and light,
Very sound of very light
Heard from morning's rosiest height,
When the soul of all delight
Fills a child's clear laughter.

Golden bells of welcome rolled
Never forth such notes, nor told
Hours so blithe in tones so bold,
As the radiant mouth of gold
Here that rings forth heaven.
If the golden-crested wren
Were a nightingale — why, then,
Something seen and heard of men
Might be half as sweet as when
Laughs a child of seven.

Algernon Charles Swinburne

A Question

Why is it, God, that mothers' hearts are made
So very deep and wide?
How does it help the world that we should hold
Such swelling floods of pain till we are old,
Because when we were young one grave was laid —
One baby died?

Charlotte Perkins Gilman

Sweet And Low

Sweet and low, sweet and low,
Wind of the western sea,
Low, low, breathe and blow,
Wind of the western sea!
Over the rolling waters go,
Come from the dying moon, and blow,
Blow him again to me;
While my little one, while my pretty one, sleeps.

Sleep and rest, sleep and rest,
Father will come to thee soon;
Rest, rest, on mother's breast,
Father will come to thee soon;
Father will come to his babe in the nest,
Silver sails all out of the west,
Under the silver moon:
Sleep, my little one, sleep, my pretty one, sleep.

Alfred, Lord Tennyson

The Children's Hour

Between the dark and the daylight,
  When the night is beginning to lower,
Comes a pause in the day's occupations,
  That is known as the Children's Hour.

I hear in the chamber above me
  The patter of little feet,
The sound of a door that is opened,
  And voices soft and sweet.

From my study I see in the lamplight,
  Descending the broad hall stair,
Grave Alice, and laughing Allegra,
  And Edith with golden hair.

A whisper, and then a silence:
  Yet I know by their merry eyes
They are plotting and planning together
  To take me by surprise.

A sudden rush from the stairway,
  A sudden raid from the hall!
By three doors left unguarded
  They enter my castle wall!

They climb up into my turret
 O'er the arms and back of my chair;
If I try to escape, they surround me;
 They seem to be everywhere.

They almost devour me with kisses,
 Their arms about me entwine,
Till I think of the Bishop of Bingen
 In his Mouse-Tower on the Rhine!

Do you think, O blue-eyed banditti,
 Because you have scaled the wall,
Such an old mustache as I am
 Is not a match for you all!

I have you fast in my fortress,
 And will not let you depart,
But put you down into the dungeon
 In the round-tower of my heart.

And there will I keep you forever,
 Yes, forever and a day,
Till the walls shall crumble to ruin,
 And moulder in dust away.

Henry Wadsworth Longfellow

My Early Home

Here sparrows build upon the trees,
And stock-dove hides her nest:
The leaves are winnowed by the breeze
Into a calmer rest;
The black-cap's song was very sweet;
That used the rose to kiss;
It made the paradise complete:
My early home was this.

The redbreast from the sweetbrier bush
Dropt down to pick the worm;
On the horse-chestnut sang the thrush,
O'er the house where I was born.
The moonlight, like a shower of pearls,
Fell o'er this 'bower of bliss',
And on the bench sat boys and girls;
My early home was this.

The old house stooped just like a cave,
Thatched o'er with mosses green;
Winter around the walls would rave,
But all was calm within;
The trees are here all green again,
Here bees the flowers still kiss,
But flowers and trees seemed sweeter then;
My early home was this.

John Clare

To Flush, My Dog

Yet, my pretty sportive friend,
Little is't to such an end
That I praise thy rareness!
Other dogs may be thy peers
Haply in these drooping ears,
And this glossy fairness.

But of thee it shall be said,
This dog watched beside a bed
Day and night unweary —
Watched within a curtained room,
Where no sunbeam brake the gloom
Round the sick and dreary.

Roses, gathered for a vase,
In that chamber died apace,
Beam and breeze resigning.
This dog only, waited on,
Knowing that when light is gone
Love remains for shining.

Other dogs in thymy dew
Tracked the hares, and followed through
Sunny moor or meadow.
This dog only, crept and crept
Next a languid cheek that slept,
Sharing in the shadow.

Other dogs of loyal cheer
Bounded at the whistle clear,
Up the woodside hieing.
This dog only, watched in reach
Of a faintly uttered speech,
Or a louder sighing.

And if one or two quick tears
Dropped upon his glossy ears,
Or a sigh came double —
Up he sprang in eager haste,
Fawning, fondling, breathing fast,
In a tender trouble.

And this dog was satisfied
If a pale thin hand would glide
Down his dewlaps sloping —
Which he pushed his nose within,
After platforming his chin
On the palm left open.

Elizabeth Barrett Browning

Milk For The Cat

When the tea is brought at five o'clock,
And all the neat curtains are drawn with care,
The little black cat with bright green eyes
Is suddenly purring there.

At first she pretends, having nothing to do,
She has come in merely to blink by the grate,
But, though tea may be late or the milk may be sour,
She is never late.

And presently her agate eyes
Take a soft large milky haze,
And her independent casual glance
Becomes a stiff, hard gaze.

Then she stamps her claws or lifts her ears,
Or twists her tail and begins to stir,
Till suddenly all her lithe body becomes
One breathing, trembling purr.

The children eat and wriggle and laugh;
The two old ladies stroke their silk:
But the cat is grown small and thin with desire,
Transformed to a creeping lust for milk.

The white saucer like some full moon descends
At last from the clouds of the table above;
She sighs and dreams and thrills and glows,
Transfigured with love.

She nestles over the shining rim,
Buries her chin in the creamy sea;
Her tail hangs loose; each drowsy paw
Is doubled under each bending knee.

A long, dim ecstasy holds her life;
Her world is an infinite shapeless white,
Till her tongue has curled the last holy drop,
Then she sinks back into the night,

Draws and dips her body to heap
Her sleepy nerves in the great arm-chair,
Lies defeated and buried deep
Three or four hours unconscious there.

Harold Monro

A Visit From St. Nicholas

'Twas the night before Christmas, when all through the house
Not a creature was stirring, not even a mouse;
The stockings were hung by the chimney with care,
In hopes that St. Nicholas soon would be there;
The children were nestled all snug in their beds,
While visions of sugar-plums danced in their heads;
And mamma in her 'kerchief, and I in my cap,
Had just settled our brains for a long winter's nap,
When out on the lawn there arose such a clatter,
I sprang from the bed to see what was the matter.
Away to the window I flew like a flash,
Tore open the shutters and threw up the sash.
The moon on the breast of the new-fallen snow
Gave the lustre of mid-day to objects below,
When, what to my wondering eyes should appear,
But a miniature sleigh, and eight tiny reindeer,
With a little old driver, so lively and quick,
I knew in a moment it must be St. Nick.
More rapid than eagles his coursers they came,
And he whistled, and shouted, and called them by name;
'Now, Dasher! now, Dancer! now, Prancer and Vixen!
On, Comet! on, Cupid! on, Donder and Blitzen!
To the top of the porch! to the top of the wall!
Now dash away! dash away! dash away all!'
As dry leaves that before the wild hurricane fly,
When they meet with an obstacle, mount to the sky;
So up to the house-top the coursers they flew,
With the sleigh full of Toys, and St. Nicholas too.
And then, in a twinkling, I heard on the roof
The prancing and pawing of each little hoof.
As I drew in my head, and was turning around,

Down the chimney St. Nicholas came with a bound.
He was dressed all in fur, from his head to his foot,
And his clothes were all tarnished with ashes and soot;
A bundle of Toys he had flung on his back,
And he looked like a peddler just opening his pack.
His eyes — how they twinkled! his dimples how merry!
His cheeks were like roses, his nose like a cherry!
His droll little mouth was drawn up like a bow
And the beard of his chin was as white as the snow;
The stump of a pipe he held tight in his teeth,
And the smoke it encircled his head like a wreath;
He had a broad face and a little round belly,
That shook when he laughed, like a bowlful of jelly.
He was chubby and plump, a right jolly old elf,
And I laughed when I saw him, in spite of myself;
A wink of his eye and a twist of his head,
Soon gave me to know I had nothing to dread;
He spoke not a word, but went straight to his work,
And filled all the stockings; then turned with a jerk,
And laying his finger aside of his nose,
And giving a nod, up the chimney he rose;
He sprang to his sleigh, to his team gave a whistle,
And away they all flew like the down of a thistle,
But I heard him exclaim, ere he drove out of sight,
'Happy Christmas to all, and to all a good-night.'

Clement C. Moore

Mother To Child

How best can I serve thee, my child! My child!
Flesh of my flesh and dear heart of my heart!
Once thou wast within me — I held thee — I fed thee —
By the force of my loving and longing I led thee —
Now we are apart!

I may blind thee with kisses and crush with embracing,
Thy warm mouth in my neck and our arms interlacing;
But here in my body my soul lives alone,
And thou answerest me from a house of thine own —
The house which I builded!

Which we builded together, thy father and I;
In which thou must live, O my darling, and die!
Not one stone can I alter, one atom relay —
Not to save or defend thee or help thee to stay —
That gift is completed!

How best can I serve thee? O child, if they knew
How my heart aches with loving! How deep and how true,
How brave and enduring, how patient, how strong,
How longing for good and how fearful of wrong,
Is the love of thy mother!

Could I crown thee with riches! Surround, overflow thee
With fame and with power till the whole world should know thee;
With wisdom and genius to hold the world still,
To bring laughter and tears, joy and pain, at thy will,
Still — thou mightst not be happy!

Such have lived — and in sorrow. The greater the mind
The wider and deeper the grief it can find.
The richer, the gladder, the more thou canst feel
The keen stings that a lifetime is sure to reveal.
O my child! Must thou suffer?

Is there no way my life can save thine from a pain?
Is the love of a mother no possible gain?
No labor of Hercules — search for the Grail —
No way for this wonderful love to avail?
God in Heaven — O teach me!

My prayer has been answered. The pain thou must bear
Is the pain of the world's life which thy life must share,
Thou art one with the world — though I love thee the best;
And to save thee from pain I must save all the rest —
Well — with God's help I'll do it.

Thou art one with the rest. I must love thee in them.
Thou wilt sin with the rest; and thy mother must stem
The world's sin. Thou wilt weep, and thy mother must dry
The tears of the world lest her darling should cry.
I will do it — God helping!

And I stand not alone. I will gather a band
Of all loving mothers from land unto land.
Our children are part of the world! Do ye hear?
They are one with the world — we must hold them all dear!
Love all for the child's sake!

For the sake of my child I must hasten to save
All the children on earth from the jail and the grave.
For so, and so only, I lighten the share
Of the pain of the world that my darling must bear —
Even so, and so only!

Charlotte Perkins Gilman

It Is A Beauteous Evening

It is a beauteous evening, calm and free,
The holy time is quiet as a nun
Breathless with adoration; the broad sun
Is sinking down in its tranquillity;
The gentleness of heaven broods o'er the sea:
Listen! the mighty Being is awake,
And doth with his eternal motion make

A sound like thunder — everlastingly.
Dear Child! dear Girl! that walkest with me here,
If thou appear untouched by solemn thought,
Thy nature is not therefore less divine:
Thou liest in Abraham's bosom all the year,
And worship'st at the Temple's inner shrine,
God being with thee when we know it not.

William Wordsworth

Mother o' Mine

If I were hanged on the highest hill,
Mother o' mine, O mother o' mine!
I know whose love would follow me still,
Mother o' mine, O mother o' mine!

If I were drowned in the deepest sea,
Mother o' mine, O mother o' mine!
I know whose tears would come down to me,
Mother o' mine, O mother o' mine!

If I were damned of body and soul,
I know whose prayers would make me whole,
Mother o' mine, O mother o' mine!

Rudyard Kipling

My Grandmother's Love Letters

There are no stars to-night
But those of memory.
Yet how much room for memory there is
In the loose girdle of soft rain.

There is even room enough
For the letters of my mother's mother,
Elizabeth,
That have been pressed so long
Into a corner of the roof
That they are brown and soft,
And liable to melt as snow.

Over the greatness of such space
Steps must be gentle.
It is all hung by an invisible white hair.
It trembles as birch limbs webbing the air.

And I ask myself:

'Are your fingers long enough to play
Old keys that are but echoes:
Is the silence strong enough
To carry back the music to its source
And back to you again
As though to her?'

Yet I would lead my grandmother by the hand
Through much of what she would not understand;
And so I stumble. And the rain continues on the roof
With such a sound of gently pitying laughter.

Hart Crane

The First Snow-Fall

The snow had begun in the gloaming,
    And busily all the night
Had been heaping field and highway
    With a silence deep and white.

Every pine and fir and hemlock
    Wore ermine too dear for an earl,
And the poorest twig on the elm-tree
    Was ridged inch deep with pearl.

From sheds new-roofed with Carrara
    Came Chanticleer's muffled crow,
The stiff rails softened to swan's-down,
    And still fluttered down the snow.

I stood and watched by the window
    The noiseless work of the sky,
And the sudden flurries of snow-birds,
    Like brown leaves whirling by.

I thought of a mound in sweet Auburn
    Where a little headstone stood;
How the flakes were folding it gently,
    As did robins the babes in the wood.

Up spoke our own little Mabel,
   Saying, 'Father, who makes it snow?'
And I told of the good All-father
   Who cares for us here below.

Again I looked at the snowfall,
   And thought of the leaden sky
That arched o'er our first great sorrow,
   When that mound was heaped so high.

I remembered the gradual patience
   That fell from that cloud like snow,
Flake by flake, healing and hiding
   The scar of our deep-plunged woe.

And again to the child I whispered,
   'The snow that husheth all,
Darling, the merciful Father
   Alone can make it fall!'

Then, with eyes that saw not, I kissed her;
   And she, kissing back, could not know
That my kiss was given to her sister,
   Folded close under deepening snow.

James Russell Lowell

To My Mother

Because I feel that, in the Heavens above,
The angels, whispering to one another,
Can find, among their burning terms of love,
None so devotional as that of 'Mother,'
Therefore by that dear name I long have called you —
You who are more than mother unto me,
And fill my heart of hearts, where Death installed you
In setting my Virginia's spirit free.
My mother– my own mother, who died early,
Was but the mother of myself; but you
Are mother to the one I loved so dearly,
And thus are dearer than the mother I knew
By that infinity with which my wife
Was dearer to my soul than its soul-life.

Edgar Allan Poe

Marriage

The die is cast, come weal, come woe,
Two lives are joined together,
For better or for worse, the link
Which naught but death can sever.
The die is cast, come grief, come joy,
Come richer, or come poorer,
If love but binds the mystic tie,
Blest is the bridal hour.

Mary Weston Fordham

On His Deceased Wife

Methought I saw my late espoused Saint
  Brought to me like Alcestis from the grave,
  Who Jove's great Son to her glad Husband gave,
  Rescu'd from death by force though pale and faint.
Mine as whom washt from spot of child-bed taint
  Purification in the old Law did save,
  And such as yet once more I trust to have
  Full sight of her in Heav'n without restraint,
Came vested all in white, pure as her mind:
  Her face was veil'd, yet to my fancied sight
  Love, sweetness, goodness in her person shin'd
So clear, as in no face with more delight.
  But O as to embrace me she enclin'd
  I wak'd, she fled, and day brought back my night.

John Milton

A Tragedy

I
Among his books he sits all day
To think and read and write;
He does not smell the new-mown hay,
The roses red and white.

I walk among them all alone,
His silly, stupid wife;
The world seems tasteless, dead and done —
An empty thing is life.

At night his window casts a square
Of light upon the lawn;
I sometimes walk and watch it there
Until the chill of dawn.

I have no brain to understand
The books he loves to read;
I only have a heart and hand
He does not seem to need.

He calls me 'Child' — lays on my hair
Thin fingers, cold and mild;
Oh! God of Love, who answers prayer,
I wish I were a child!

And no one sees and no one knows
(He least would know or see),
That ere Love gathers next year's rose
Death will have gathered me.

And on my grave will bindweed pink
And round-faced daisies grow:
He still will read and write and think,
And never, never know!

II
It's lonely in my study here alone,
Now you are gone:
I loved to see your white gown 'mid the
flowers,
While hours on hours
I studied—toiled to weave a crown of fame
About your name.

I liked to hear your sweet, low laughter ring;
To hear you sing
About the house while I sat reading here,
My child, my dear;
To know you glad with all the life-joys fair
I dared not share.

I thought there would be time enough to show
My love, you know,
When I could lay with laurels at your feet
Love's roses sweet;
I thought I could taste love when fame was won—
Now both are done!

Thank God, your child-heart knew not how to
miss
The passionate kiss
Which I dared never give, lest love should rise
Mighty, unwise,
And bind me, with my life-work incomplete,
Beside your feet.

You never knew, you lived and were content:
My one chance went;
You died, my little one, and are at rest—
And I, unblest,
Look at these broken fragments of my life,
My child, my wife.

Edith Nesbit

The Voice

Woman much missed, how you call to me, call to me,
Saying that now you are not as you were
When you had changed from the one who was all to me,
But as at first, when our day was fair.

Can it be you that I hear? Let me view you, then,
Standing as when I drew near to the town
Where you would wait for me: yes, as I knew you then,
Even to the original air-blue gown!

Or is it only the breeze, in its listlessness
Travelling across the wet mead to me here,
You being ever dissolved to wan wistlessness,
Heard no more again far or near?

Thus I; faltering forward,
Leaves around me falling,
Wind oozing thin through the thorn from norward,
And the woman calling.

Thomas Hardy

To My Dear and Loving Husband

If ever two were one, then surely we.
If ever man were lov'd by wife, then thee.
If ever wife was happy in a man,
Compare with me, ye women, if you can.

I prize thy love more than whole Mines of gold
Or all the riches that the East doth hold.
My love is such that Rivers cannot quench,
Nor aught but love from thee give recompense.

Thy love is such I can no way repay.
The heavens reward thee manifold, I pray.
Then while we live, in love let's so persever
That when we live no more, we may live ever.

Anne Bradstreet

The Widower

For a season there must be pain —
For a little, little space
I shall lose the sight of her face,
Take back the old life again
While She is at rest in her place.

For a season this pain must endure,
For a little, little while
I shall sigh more often than smile
Till time shall work me a cure,
And the pitiful days beguile.

For that season we must be apart,
For a little length of years,
Till my life's last hour nears,
And, above the beat of my heart,
I hear Her voice in my ears.

But I shall not understand —
Being set on some later love,
Shall not know her for whom I strove,
Till she reach me forth her hand,
Saying, 'Who but I have the right?'
And out of a troubled night
Shall draw me safe to the land.

Rudyard Kipling

An Epitaph Upon Husband and Wife

To these whom death again did wed
This grave's the second marriage-bed.
For though the hand of Fate could force
'Twixt soul and body a divorce,
It could not sunder man and wife,
Because they both lived but one life.
Peace, good reader, do not weep;
Peace, the lovers are asleep.
They, sweet turtles, folded lie
In the last knot that love could tie.
And though they lie as they were dead,
Their pillow stone, their sheets of lead,
(Pillow hard, and sheets not warm)
Love made the bed; they'll take no harm.
Let them sleep, let them sleep on,
Till the stormy night be gone,
And the eternal morrow dawn;
Then the curtains will be drawn,
And they wake into a light
Whose day shall never die in night.

Richard Crashaw

Winter Evening

Now stir the fire, and close the shutters fast,
Let fall the curtains, wheel the sofa round,
And, while the bubbling and loud-hissing urn
Throws up a steamy column, and the cups,
That cheer but not inebriate, wait on each,
So let us welcome peaceful ev'ning in...
Oh winter, ruler of th' inverted year...
I love thee, all unlovely as thou seem'st,
And dreaded as thou art! Thou hold'st the sun
A pris'ner in the yet undawning east,
Short'ning his journey between morn and noon,
And hurrying him, impatient of his stay,
Down to the rosy west; but kindly still
Compensating his loss with added hours
Of social converse and instructive ease,
And gath'ring, at short notice, in one group
The family dispers'd, and fixing thought,
Not less dispers'd by day-light and its cares.
I crown thee king of intimate delights,
Fire-side enjoyments, home-born happiness,
And all the comforts that the lowly roof
Of undisturb'd retirement, and the hours
Of long uninterrupted ev'ning, know.

William Cowper

The Old Vicarage, Grantchester

Just now the lilac is in bloom,
All before my little room;
And in my flower-beds, I think,
Smile the carnation and the pink;
And down the borders, well I know,
The poppy and the pansy blow . . .
Oh! there the chestnuts, summer through,
Beside the river make for you
A tunnel of green gloom, and sleep
Deeply above; and green and deep
The stream mysterious glides beneath,
Green as a dream and deep as death.
  — Oh, damn! I know it! and I know
How the May fields all golden show,
And when the day is young and sweet,
Gild gloriously the bare feet
That run to bathe . . .
          Du lieber Gott!

Here am I, sweating, sick, and hot,
And there the shadowed waters fresh
Lean up to embrace the naked flesh.
Temperanmentvoll German Jews
Drink beer around; — and *there* the dews
Are soft beneath a morn of gold.
Here tulips bloom as they are told;
Unkempt about those hedges blows
An English unofficial rose;
And there the unregulated sun

Slopes down to rest when day is done,
And wakes a vague unpunctual star,
A slippered Hesper; and there are
Meads towards Haslingfield and Coton
Where *das Betreten's* not *verboten*.

ἐῖθε γενοίμην ... would I were
In Grantchester, in Grantchester! –
Some, it may be, can get in touch
With Nature there, or Earth, or such.
And clever modern men have seen
A Faun a-peeping through the green,
And felt the Classics were not dead,
To glimpse a Naiad's reedy head,
Or hear the Goat-foot piping low: ...
But these are things I do not know.
I only know that you may lie
Day-long and watch the Cambridge sky,
And, flower-lulled in sleepy grass,
Hear the cool lapse of hours pass,
Until the centuries blend and blur
In Grantchester, in Grantchester ...
Still in the dawnlit waters cool
His ghostly Lordship swims his pool,
And tries the strokes, essays the tricks,
Long learnt on Hellespont, or Styx.
Dan Chaucer hears his river still
Chatter beneath a phantom mill.
Tennyson notes, with studious eye,

How Cambridge waters hurry by . . .
And in that garden, black and white,
Creep whispers through the grass all night;
And spectral dance, before the dawn,
A hundred Vicars down the lawn;
Curates, long dust, will come and go
On lissom, clerical, printless toe;
And oft between the boughs is seen
The sly shade of a Rural Dean . . .
Till, at a shiver in the skies,
Vanishing with Satanic cries,
The prim ecclesiastic rout
Leaves but a startled sleeper-out,
Grey heavens, the first bird's drowsy calls,
The falling house that never falls.

God! I will pack, and take a train,
And get me to England once again!
For England's the one land, I know,
Where men with Splendid Hearts may go;
And Cambridgeshire, of all England,
The shire for Men who Understand;
And of *that* district I prefer
The lovely hamlet Grantchester.
For Cambridge people rarely smile,
Being urban, swaut, and packed with guile;
And Royston men in the far South
Are black and fierce and strange of mouth;
At Over they fling oaths at one,

And worse than oaths at Trumpington,
And Ditton girls are mean and dirty,
And there's none in Harston under thirty,
And folks in Shelford and those parts
Have twisted lips and twisted hearts.
And Barton men make Cockney rhymes,
And Coton's full of nameless crimes,
And things are done you'd not believe
At Madingley, on Christmas Eve.
Strong men have run for miles and miles,
When one from Cherry Hinton smiles;
Strong men have blanched, and shot their wives,
Rather than send them to St. Ives;
Strong men have cried like babes, bydam,
To hear what happened at Babraham.
But Grantchester! ah, Grantchester!
There's peace and holy quiet there,
Great clouds along pacific skies,
And men and women with straight eyes,
Lithe children lovelier than a dream,
A bosky wood, a slumberous stream,
And little kindly winds that creep
Round twilight corners, half asleep.
In Grantchester their skins are white;
They bathe by day, they bathe by night;
The women there do all they ought;
The men observe the Rules of Thought.
They love the Good; they worship Truth;
They laugh uproariously in youth;

(And when they get to feeling old,
They up and shoot themselves, I'm told)...

Ah God! to see the branches stir
Across the moon at Grantchester!
To smell the thrilling-sweet and rotten
Unforgettable, unforgotten
River-smell, and hear the breeze
Sobbing in the little trees.
Say, do the elm-clumps greatly stand
Still guardians of that holy land?
The chestnuts shade, in reverend dream,
The yet unacademic stream?
Is dawn a secret shy and cold
Anadyomene, silver-gold?
And sunset still a golden sea
From Haslingfield to Madingley?
And after, ere the night is born,
Do hares come out about the corn?
Oh, is the water sweet and cool,
Gentle and brown, above the pool?
And laughs the immortal river still
Under the mill, under the mill?
Say, is there Beauty yet to find?
And Certainty? and Quiet kind?
Deep meadows yet, for to forget
The lies, and truths, and pain?... oh! yet
Stands the Church clock at ten to three?
And is there honey still for tea?

Rupert Brooke

To My Daughter Betty, The Gift Of God

In wiser days, my darling rosebud, blown
To beauty proud as was your mother's prime,
In that desired, delayed, incredible time,
You'll ask why I abandoned you, my own,
And the dear heart that was your baby throne,
To dice with death. And oh! they'll give you rhyme
And reason: some will call the thing sublime,
And some decry it in a knowing tone.
So here, while the mad guns curse overhead,
And tired men sigh with mud for couch and floor,
Know that we fools, now with the foolish dead,
Died not for flag, nor King, nor Emperor,
But for a dream, born in a herdsman's shed,
And for the secret Scripture of the poor.

T. M. Kettle

Love and Romance

Loving In Truth, And Fain In Verse
My Love To Show

Loving in truth, and fain in verse my love to show,
That She, dear She, might take some pleasure of my pain,
Pleasure might cause her read, reading might make her know,
Knowledge might pity win, and pity grace obtain,
I sought fit words to paint the blackest face of woe,
Studying inventions fine, her wits to entertain,
Oft turning others' leaves, to see if thence would flow
Some fresh and fruitful showers upon my sunburnt brain.
But words came halting forth, wanting Invention's stay;
Invention, Nature's child, fled step-dame Study's blows;
And others' feet still seemed but strangers in my way.
Thus, great with child to speak, and helpless in my throes,
Biting my truant pen, beating myself for spite:
'Fool!' said my Muse to me, 'Look in thy heart, and write!'

Sir Philip Sidney

How Do I Love Thee?
Let Me Count The Ways

How do I love thee? Let me count the ways.
I love thee to the depth and breadth and height
My soul can reach, when feeling out of sight
For the ends of Being and ideal Grace.
I love thee to the level of everyday's
Most quiet need, by sun and candlelight.
I love thee freely, as men strive for Right;
I love thee purely, as they turn from Praise.
I love thee with the passion put to use
In my old griefs, and with my childhood's faith.
I love thee with a love I seemed to lose
With my lost saints, — I love thee with the breath,
Smiles, tears, of all my life! — and, if God choose,
I shall but love thee better after death.

Elizabeth Barrett Browning

The Garden Of Love

I went to the Garden of Love,
And saw what I never had seen;
A Chapel was built in the midst,
Where I used to play on the green.

And the gates of this Chapel were shut,
And 'Thou shalt not' writ over the door;
So I turned to the Garden of Love
That so many sweet flowers bore.

And I saw it was filled with graves,
And tombstones where flowers should be;
And priests in black gowns were walking their rounds,
And binding with briars my joys and desires.

William Blake

My Luve's Like A Red, Red Rose

O my Luve's like a red, red rose,
That's newly sprung in June:
O my Luve's like the melodie,
That's sweetly played in tune.

As fair art thou, my bonnie lass,
So deep in luve am I;
And I will luve thee still, my dear,
Till a' the seas gang dry.

Till a' the seas gang dry, my dear,
And the rocks melt wi' the sun;
I will luve thee still, my dear,
While the sands o' life shall run.

And fare-thee-weel, my only Luve!
And fare-thee-weel, a while!
And I will come again, my Luve,
Tho' 'twere ten thousand mile!

Robert Burns

Go, Lovely Rose

Go, lovely rose!
Tell her that wastes her time and me,
That now she knows,
When I resemble her to thee,
How sweet and fair she seems to be.

Tell her that's young,
And shuns to have her graces spied,
That hadst thou sprung
In deserts where no men abide,
Thou must have uncommended died.

Small is the worth
Of beauty from the light retired;
Bid her come forth,
Suffer herself to be desired,
And not blush so to be admired.

Then die! that she
The common fate of all things rare
May read in thee;
How small a part of time they share
That are so wondrous sweet and fair.

Edmund Waller

Cherry-Ripe

There is a garden in her face
Where roses and white lilies grow;
A heavenly paradise is that place,
Wherein all pleasant fruits do flow:
  There cherries grow which none may buy
  Till 'Cherry-ripe' themselves do cry.

Those cherries fairly do enclose
Of orient pearl a double row,
Which when her lovely laughter shows,
They look like rose-buds fill'd with snow;
  Yet them nor peer nor prince can buy
  Till 'Cherry-ripe' themselves do cry.

Her eyes like angels watch them still;
Her brows like bended bows do stand,
Threat'ning with piercing frowns to kill
All that attempt with eye or hand
  Those sacred cherries to come nigh,
  Till 'Cherry-ripe' themselves do cry.

Thomas Campion

She Walks In Beauty

She walks in beauty, like the night
    Of cloudless climes and starry skies;
And all that's best of dark and bright
    Meet in her aspect and her eyes:
Thus mellowed to that tender light
    Which heaven to gaudy day denies.

One shade the more, one ray the less,
    Had half impaired the nameless grace
Which waves in every raven tress,
    Or softly lightens o'er her face;
Where thoughts serenely sweet express
    How pure, how dear their dwelling-place.

And on that cheek, and o'er that brow,
    So soft, so calm, yet eloquent,
The smiles that win, the tints that glow,
    But tell of days in goodness spent,
A mind at peace with all below,
    A heart whose love is innocent!

George Gordon, Lord Byron

Love's Philosophy

The Fountains mingle with the river
And the rivers with the ocean,
The winds of heaven mix for ever
With a sweet emotion;
Nothing in the world is single,
All things by a law divine
In one another's being mingle —
Why not I with thine?

See the mountains kiss high heaven
And the waves clasp one another;
No sister-flower would be forgiven
If it disdain'd its brother:
And the sunlight clasps the earth,
And the moonbeams kiss the sea —
What are all these kissings worth,
If thou kiss not me?

Percy Bysshe Shelley

One Day I Wrote Her Name Upon The Strand

One day I wrote her name upon the strand,
But came the waves and washed it away:
Again I wrote it with a second hand,
But came the tide, and made my pains his prey.
Vain man, said she, that dost in vain assay
A mortal thing so to immortalize!
For I myself shall like to this decay,
And eke my name be wiped out likewise.
Not so quoth I, let baser things devise
To die in dust, but you shall live by fame:
My verse your virtues rare shall eternize,
And in the heavens write your glorious name;
Where, whenas death shall all the world subdue,
Our love shall live, and later life renew.

Edmund Spenser

The Good-Morrow

I wonder, by my troth, what thou and I
Did, till we loved? Were we not weaned till then?
But sucked on country pleasures, childishly?
Or snorted we in the seven sleepers' den?
'Twas so; but this, all pleasures fancies be.
If ever any beauty I did see,
Which I desired, and got, 'twas but a dream of thee.

And now good-morrow to our waking souls,
Which watch not one another out of fear;
For love, all love of other sights controls,
And makes one little room an everywhere.
Let sea-discoverers to new worlds have gone,
Let maps to other, worlds on worlds have shown,
Let us possess one world, each hath one, and is one.

My face in thine eye, thine in mine appears,
And true plain hearts do in the faces rest;
Where can we find two better hemispheres
Without sharp North, without declining West?
Whatever dies was not mixed equally;
If our two loves be one, or thou and I
Love so alike that none do slacken, none can die.

John Donne

The Clod And The Pebble

'Love seeketh not itself to please,
Nor for itself hath any care,
But for another gives its ease,
And builds a heaven in hell's despair.'

So sung a little clod of clay,
Trodden with the cattle's feet,
But a pebble of the brook
Warbled out these metres meet:

'Love seeketh only Self to please,
To bind another to its delight,
Joys in another's loss of ease,
And builds a hell in heaven's despite.'

William Blake

The Sun Rising

Busy old fool, unruly Sun,
Why dost thou thus,
Through windows, and through curtains, call on us?
Must to thy motions lovers' seasons run?
Saucy pedantic wretch, go chide
Late school-boys and sour prentices,
Go tell court-huntsmen that the king will ride,
Call country ants to harvest offices;
Love, all alike, no season knows nor clime,
Nor hours, days, months, which are the rags of time.

Thy beams so reverend, and strong
Why shouldst thou think?
I could eclipse and cloud them with a wink,
But that I would not lose her sight so long.
If her eyes have not blinded thine,
Look, and to-morrow late tell me,
Whether both th' Indias of spice and mine
Be where thou left'st them, or lie here with me.
Ask for those kings whom thou saw'st yesterday,
And thou shalt hear, 'All here in one bed lay.'

She's all states, and all princes, I;
Nothing else is;
Princes do but play us; compared to this,
All honour's mimic, all wealth alchemy.
Thou, Sun, art half as happy as we,
In that the world's contracted thus;
Thine age asks ease, and since thy duties be
To warm the world, that's done in warming us.
Shine here to us, and thou art everywhere;
This bed thy center is, these walls thy sphere.

John Donne

You Smiled, You Spoke And I Believed

You smiled, you spoke and I believed,
By every word and smile – deceived.
Another man would hope no more;
Nor hope I – what I hoped before.
But let not this last wish be vain;
Deceive, deceive me once again!

Walter Savage Landor

The Definition Of Love

My Love is of a birth as rare
As 'tis, for object, strange and high;
It was begotten by Despair,
Upon Impossibility.

Magnanimous Despair alone
Could show me so divine a thing,
Where feeble hope could ne'er have flown,
But vainly flapped its tinsel wing.

And yet I quickly might arrive
Where my extended soul is fixed;
But Fate does iron wedges drive,
And always crowds itself betwixt.

For Fate with jealous eye does see
Two perfect loves, nor lets them close;
Their union would her ruin be,
And her tyrannic power depose.

And therefore her decrees of steel
Us as the distant poles have placed,
(Though Love's whole world on us doth wheel),
Not by themselves to be embraced,

Unless the giddy heaven fall,
And earth some new convulsion tear.
And, us to join, the world should all
Be cramp'd into a planisphere.

As lines, so Love's oblique, may well
Themselves in every angle greet:
But ours, so truly parallel,
Though infinite, can never meet.

Therefore the Love which us doth bind,
But Fate so enviously debars,
Is the conjunction of the mind,
And opposition of the stars.

Andrew Marvell

To Celia

Drink to me only with thine eyes,
And I will pledge with mine;
Or leave a kiss but in the cup
And I'll not look for wine.
The thirst that from the soul doth rise
Doth ask a drink divine;
But might I of Jove's nectar sup,
I would not change for thine.

I sent thee late a rosy wreath,
Not so much honouring thee
As giving it a hope that there
It could not wither'd be;
But thou thereon didst only breathe,
And sent'st it back to me;
Since when it grows, and smells, I swear,
Not of itself but thee!

Ben Jonson

Severed Selves

Two separate divided silences,
Which, brought together, would find loving voice;
Two glances which together would rejoice
In love, now lost like stars beyond dark trees;
Two hands apart whose touch alone gives ease;
Two bosoms which, heart-shrined with mutual flame,
Would, meeting in one clasp, be made the same;
Two souls, the shores wave-mocked of sundering seas: —
Such are we now. Ah! may our hope forecast
Indeed one hour again, when on this stream
Of darkened love once more the light shall gleam? —
An hour how slow to come, how quickly past, —
Which blooms and fades, and only leaves at last,
Faint as shed flowers, the attenuated dream.

Dante Gabriel Rossetti

Love's Secret

Never seek to tell thy love,
Love that never told can be;
For the gentle wind doth move
Silently, invisibly.

I told my love, I told my love,
I told her all my heart,
Trembling, cold, in ghastly fears.
Ah! she did depart!
Soon after she was gone from me,
A traveller came by,
Silently, invisibly:
He took her with a sigh.

William Blake

To My Inconstant Mistress

When thou, poor excommunicate
    From all the joys of love, shalt see
The full reward and glorious fate
    Which my strong faith shall purchase me,
    Then curse thine own inconstancy.

A fairer hand than thine shall cure
    That heart which thy false oaths did wound;
And to my soul a soul more pure
    Than thine shall by Love's hand be bound,
    And both with equal glory crowned.

Then shalt thou weep, entreat, complain
    To Love, as I did once to thee;
When all thy tears shall be as vain
    As mine were then, for thou shalt be
    Damned for thy false apostasy.

Thomas Carew

The Appeal

And wilt thou leave me thus!
Say nay, say nay, for shame!
— To save thee from the blame
Of all my grief and grame.
And wilt thou leave me thus?
      Say nay! say nay!

And wilt thou leave me thus,
That hath loved thee so long
In wealth and woe among:
And is thy heart so strong
As for to leave me thus?
      Say nay! say nay!

And wilt thou leave me thus,
That hath given thee my heart
Never for to depart
Neither for pain nor smart:
And wilt thou leave me thus?
      Say nay! say nay!

And wilt thou leave me thus,
And have no more pitye
Of him that loveth thee?
Alas, thy cruelty!
And wilt thou leave me thus?
      Say nay! say nay!

Sir Thomas Wyatt

His Lady's Cruelty

With how sad steps, O moon, thou climb'st the skies!
How silently, and with how wan a face!
What! may it be that even in heavenly place
That busy archer his sharp arrows tries?
Sure, if that long-with-love-acquainted eyes
Can judge of love, thou feel'st a lover's case:
I read it in thy looks; thy languish'd grace
To me, that feel the like, thy state descries.
Then, even of fellowship, O moon, tell me,
Is constant love deem'd there but want of wit?
Are beauties there as proud as here they be?
Do they above love to be loved, and yet
       Those lovers scorn whom that love doth possess?
       Do they call 'virtue' there — ungratefulness?

Sir Philip Sidney

Carrier Letter

My hands have not touched water since your hands, —
No; — nor my lips freed laughter since 'farewell'.
And with the day, distance again expands
Between us, voiceless as an uncoiled shell.

Yet, — much follows, much endures... Trust birds alone:
A dove's wings clung about my heart last night
With surging gentleness; and the blue stone
Set in the tryst-ring has but worn more bright.

Hart Crane

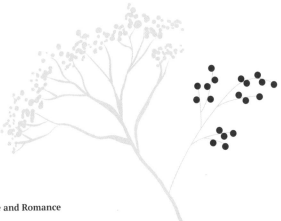

Let Me Not To The Marriage Of True Minds

Let me not to the marriage of true minds
Admit impediments. Love is not love
Which alters when it alteration finds,
Or bends with the remover to remove:
O no! it is an ever-fixèd mark
That looks on tempests and is never shaken;
It is the star to every wandering bark,
Whose worth's unknown, although his height be taken.
Love's not Time's fool, though rosy lips and cheeks
Within his bending sickle's compass come:
Love alters not with his brief hours and weeks,
But bears it out even to the edge of doom.
     If this be error and upon me proved,
     I never writ, nor no man ever loved.

William Shakespeare

To His Coy Mistress

Had we but world enough, and time,
This coyness, lady, were no crime.
We would sit down and think which way
To walk, and pass our long love's day;
Thou by the Indian Ganges' side
Shouldst rubies find; I by the tide
Of Humber would complain. I would
Love you ten years before the Flood;
And you should, if you please, refuse
Till the conversion of the Jews.
My vegetable love should grow
Vaster than empires, and more slow.
An hundred years should go to praise
Thine eyes, and on thy forehead gaze;
Two hundred to adore each breast,
But thirty thousand to the rest;
An age at least to every part,
And the last age should show your heart.
For, lady, you deserve this state,
Nor would I love at lower rate.

But at my back I always hear
Time's winged chariot hurrying near;
And yonder all before us lie

Deserts of vast eternity.
Thy beauty shall no more be found,
Nor, in thy marble vault, shall sound
My echoing song; then worms shall try
That long preserv'd virginity,
And your quaint honour turn to dust,
And into ashes all my lust.
The grave's a fine and private place,
But none I think do there embrace.

Now therefore, while the youthful hue
Sits on thy skin like morning dew,
And while thy willing soul transpires
At every pore with instant fires,
Now let us sport us while we may;
And now, like am'rous birds of prey,
Rather at once our time devour,
Than languish in his slow-chapp'd power.
Let us roll all our strength, and all
Our sweetness, up into one ball;
And tear our pleasures with rough strife
Thorough the iron gates of life.
Thus, though we cannot make our sun
Stand still, yet we will make him run.

Andrew Marvell

Silent Noon

Your hands lie open in the long fresh grass, —
The finger-points look through like rosy blooms:
Your eyes smile peace. The pasture gleams and glooms
'Neath billowing skies that scatter and amass.
All round our nest, far as the eye can pass,
Are golden kingcup-fields with silver edge
Where the cow-parsley skirts the hawthorn-hedge.
'Tis visible silence, still as the hour-glass.

Deep in the sun-searched growths the dragon-fly
Hangs like a blue thread loosened from the sky: —
So this wing'd hour is dropt to us from above.
Oh! clasp we to our hearts, for deathless dower,
This close-companioned inarticulate hour
When twofold silence was the song of love.

Dante Gabriel Rossetti

At The Mid Hour Of Night

At the mid hour of night, when stars are weeping, I fly
To the lone vale we lov'd, when life shone warm in thine eye;
    And I think oft, if spirits can steal from the regions of air,
      To revisit past scenes of delight, thou wilt come to me there,
And tell me our love is remember'd, ev'n in the sky.

Then I sing the wild song, 'twas once such rapture to hear
When our voices commingling, breath'd like one on the ear;
    And, as echo far off through the vale my sad orison rolls,
      I think, oh my love! 'tis thy voice from the kingdom of souls
Faintly answering still the notes that once were so dear.

Thomas Moore

The First Day

I wish I could remember the first day,
First hour, first moment of your meeting me,
If bright or dim the season, it might be
Summer or winter for aught I can say;
So unrecorded did it slip away,
So blind was I to see and to foresee,
So dull to mark the budding of my tree
That would not blossom, yet, for many a May.
If only I could recollect it. such
A day of days! I let it come and go
As traceless as a thaw of bygone snow;
It seemed to mean so little, meant so much;
If only now I could recall that touch,
First touch of hand in hand — Did one, but know!

Christina Georgina Rossetti

Bright Star,
Would I Were Steadfast As Thou Art

Bright star, would I were steadfast as thou art —
      Not in lone splendour hung aloft the night
And watching, with eternal lids apart,
      Like nature's patient, sleepless Eremite,
The moving waters at their priestlike task
      Of pure ablution round earth's human shores,
Or gazing on the new soft-fallen mask
      Of snow upon the mountains and the moors —
No — yet still steadfast, still unchangeable,
      Pillow'd upon my fair love's ripening breast,
To feel for ever its soft fall and swell,
      Awake for ever in a sweet unrest,
Still, still to hear her tender-taken breath,
And so live ever — or else swoon to death.

John Keats

Shall I Compare Thee To A Summer's Day?

Shall I compare thee to a summer's day?
Thou art more lovely and more temperate:
Rough winds do shake the darling buds of May,
And summer's lease hath all too short a date:
Sometime too hot the eye of heaven shines,
And often is his gold complexion dimm'd;
And every fair from fair sometime declines,
By chance, or nature's changing course, untrimm'd;
But thy eternal summer shall not fade,
Nor lose possession of that fair thou owest;
Nor shall Death brag thou wander'st in his shade,
When in eternal lines to time thou growest;
    So long as men can breathe, or eyes can see,
    So long lives this, and this gives life to thee.

William Shakespeare

False Though She Be

False though she be to me and love,
   I'll ne'er pursue revenge;
For still the charmer I approve,
   Though I deplore her change.

In hours of bliss we oft have met:
   They could not always last;
And though the present I regret,
   I'm grateful for the past.

William Congreve

My Mistress' Eyes
Are Nothing Like The Sun

My mistress' eyes are nothing like the sun;
Coral is far more red than her lips' red;
If snow be white, why then her breasts are dun;
If hairs be wires, black wires grow on her head.
I have seen roses damask'd, red and white,
But no such roses see I in her cheeks;
And in some perfumes is there more delight
Than in the breath tha d from my mistress reeks.
I love to hear her speak, yet well I know
That music hath a far more pleasing sound;
I grant I never saw a goddess go;
My mistress, when she walks, treads on the ground.
    And yet, by heaven, I think my love as rare
    As any she belied with false compare.

William Shakespeare

Without Her

What of her glass without her? The blank grey
    There where the pool is blind of the moon's face.
    Her dress without her? The tossed empty space
Of cloud-rack when the moon has passed away.
Her paths without her? Day's appointed sway
    Usurped by desolate night. Her pillowed place
    Without her? Tears, ah me! For love's good grace,
And cold forgetfulness of night or day.

What of the heart without her? Nay, poor heart,
    Of thee what word remains ere speech be still?
    A wayfarer by barren ways and chill,
Steep ways and weary, without her thou art,
Where the long cloud, the long wood's counterpart,
    Sheds doubled darkness up the labouring hill.

Dante Gabriel Rossetti

Song

Go and catch a falling star,
Get with child a mandrake root,
Tell me where all past years are,
Or who cleft the devil's foot,
Teach me to hear mermaids singing,
Or to keep off envy's stinging,
And find
What wind
Serves to advance an honest mind.

If thou be'st born to strange sights,
Things invisible to see,
Ride ten thousand days and nights,
Till age snow white hairs on thee,
Thou, when thou return'st, wilt tell me,
All strange wonders that befell thee,
And swear,
No where
Lives a woman true and fair.

If thou find'st one, let me know,
Such a pilgrimage were sweet;
Yet do not, I would not go,
Though at next door we might meet,
Though she were true, when you met her,
And last, till you write your letter,
Yet she
Will be
False, ere I come, to two, or three.

John Donne

Ruth

She stood breast-high amid the corn,
Clasp'd by the golden light of morn,
Like the sweetheart of the sun,
Who many a glowing kiss had won.

On her cheek an autumn flush,
Deeply ripen'd; — such a blush
In the midst of brown was born,
Like red poppies grown with corn.

Round her eyes her tresses fell,
Which were blackest none could tell,
But long lashes veil'd a light,
That had else been all too bright.

And her hat, with shady brim,
Made her tressy forehead dim;
Thus she stood amid the stooks,
Praising God with sweetest looks:?

Sure, I said, Heav'n did not mean,
Where I reap thou shouldst but glean,
Lay thy sheaf adown and come,
Share my harvest and my home.

Thomas Hood

Now Sleeps The Crimson Petal

Now sleeps the crimson petal, now the white;
Nor waves the cypress in the palace walk;
Nor winks the gold fin in the porphyry font:
The fire-fly wakens: waken thou with me.

Now droops the milkwhite peacock like a ghost,
And like a ghost she glimmers on to me.

Now lies the Earth all Danaë to the stars,
And all thy heart lies open unto me.

Now slides the silent meteor on, and leaves
A shining furrow, as thy thoughts in me.

Now folds the lily all her sweetness up,
And slips into the bosom of the lake:
So fold thyself, my dearest, thou, and slip
Into my bosom and be lost in me.

Alfred, Lord Tennyson

Farewell, Ungrateful Traitor!

Farewell, ungrateful traitor!
    Farewell, my perjur'd swain!
Let never injur'd woman
    Believe a man again.
The pleasure of possessing
Surpasses all expressing,
But 'tis too short a blessing,
    And love too long a pain.

'Tis easy to deceive us
    In pity of your pain,
But when we love, you leave us
    To rail at you in vain.
Before we have descried it,
There is no joy beside it,
But she that once has tried it
    Will never love again.

The passion you pretended
    Was only to obtain,
But once the charm is ended,
    The charmer you disdain.
Your love by ours we measure
Till we have lost our treasure,
But dying is a pleasure
    When living is a pain.

John Dryden

A Broken Appointment

You did not come,
And marching Time drew on, and wore me numb.
Yet less for loss of your dear presence there
Than that I thus found lacking in your make
That high compassion which can overbear
Reluctance for pure loving kindness' sake
Grieved I, when, as the hope-hour stroked its sum,
You did not come.

You love not me,
And love alone can lend you loyalty;
— I know and knew it. But, unto the store
Of human deeds divine in all but name,
Was it not worth a little hour or more
To add yet this: Once you, a woman, came
To soothe a time-torn man; even though it be
You love not me?

Thomas Hardy

Elizabeth Of Bohemia

You meaner beauties of the night,
That poorly satisfy our eyes
More by your number than your light,
You common people of the skies;
What are you when the sun shall rise?

You curious chanters of the wood,
That warble forth Dame Nature's lays,
Thinking your voices understood
By your weak accents; what's your praise
When Philomel her voice shall raise?

You violets that first appear,
By your pure purple mantles known
Like the proud virgins of the year,
As if the spring were all your own;
What are you when the rose is blown?

So, when my mistress shall be seen
In form and beauty of her mind,
By virtue first, then choice, a Queen,
Tell me, if she were not design'd
Th' eclipse and glory of her kind?

Sir Henry Wotton

To Mary Unwin

Mary! I want a lyre with other strings,
Such aid from Heaven as some have feign'd they drew,
An eloquence scarce given to mortals, new
And undebased by praise of meaner things;
That ere through age or woe I shed my wings,
I may record thy worth with honour due,
In verse as musical as thou art true,
And that immortalizes whom it sings:
But thou hast little need. There is a Book
By seraphs writ with beams of heavenly light,
On which the eyes of God not rarely look,
A chronicle of actions just and bright —
   There all thy deeds, my faithful Mary, shine;
   And since thou own'st that praise, I spare thee mine.

William Cowper

Renouncement

I must not think of thee; and, tired yet strong,
    I shun the love that lurks in all delight —
    The love of thee — and in the blue heaven's height,
And in the dearest passage of a song.
Oh, just beyond the sweetest thoughts that throng
    This breast, the thought of thee waits hidden yet bright;
    But it must never, never come in sight;
I must stop short of thee the whole day long.
But when sleep comes to close each difficult day,
    When night gives pause to the long watch I keep,
And all my bonds I needs must loose apart,
Must doff my will as raiment laid away, —
    With the first dream that comes with the first sleep
I run, I run, I am gather'd to thy heart.

Alice Meynell

Meeting At Night

The grey sea and the long black land;
And the yellow half-moon large and low;
And the startled little waves that leap
In fiery ringlets from their sleep,
As I gain the cove with pushing prow,
And quench its speed i' the slushy sand.

Then a mile of warm sea-scented beach;
Three fields to cross till a farm appears;
A tap at the pane, the quick sharp scratch
And blue spurt of a lighted match,
And a voice less loud, thro' its joys and fears,
Than the two hearts beating each to each!

Robert Browning

When We Two Parted

When we two parted
    In silence and tears,
Half broken-hearted
    To sever for years,
Pale grew thy cheek and cold,
    Colder thy kiss;
Truly that hour foretold
    Sorrow to this.

The dew of the morning
    Sunk chill on my brow
It felt like the warning
    Of what I feel now.
Thy vows are all broken,
    And light is thy fame:
I hear thy name spoken,
    And share in its shame.

They name thee before me,
　　　A knell to mine ear;
A shudder comes o'er me
　　　Why wert thou so dear?
They know not I knew thee,
　　　Who knew thee too well:
Long, long shall I rue thee,
　　　Too deeply to tell.

In secret we met,
　　　In silence I grieve,
That thy heart could forget,
　　　Thy spirit deceive.
If I should meet thee
　　　After long years,
How should I greet thee?
　　　With silence and tears.

George Gordon, Lord Byron

Echo

Come to me in the silence of the night;
    Come in the speaking silence of a dream;
Come with soft rounded cheeks and eyes as bright
    As sunlight on a stream;
      Come back in tears,
O memory, hope, love of finished years.

O dream how sweet, too sweet, too bitter sweet,
    Whose wakening should have been in Paradise,
Where souls brimfull of love abide and meet;
    Where thirsting longing eyes
      Watch the slow door
That opening, letting in, lets out no more.

Yet come to me in dreams, that I may live
    My very life again tho' cold in death:
Come back to me in dreams, that I may give
    Pulse for pulse, breath for breath:
      Speak low, lean low,
As long ago, my love, how long ago.

Christina Georgina Rossetti

The Ecstasy

Where, like a pillow on a bed,
    A pregnant bank swell'd up, to rest
The violet's reclining head,
    Sat we two, one another's best.

Our hands were firmly cemented
    With a fast balm, which thence did spring;
Our eye-beams twisted, and did thread
    Our eyes upon one double string.

So to intergraft our hands, as yet
    Was all the means to make us one ;
And pictures in our eyes to get
    Was all our propagation.

As, 'twixt two equal armies, Fate
    Suspends uncertain victory,
Our souls — which to advance their state,
    Were gone out — hung 'twixt her and me.

And whilst our souls negotiate there,
    We like sepulchral statues lay;
All day, the same our postures were,
    And we said nothing, all the day.

If any, so by love refined,
     That he soul's language understood,
And by good love were grown all mind,
     Within convenient distance stood,

He — though he knew not which soul spake,
     Because both meant, both spake the same —
Might thence a new concoction take,
     And part far purer than he came.

This ecstasy doth unperplex
     (We said) and tell us what we love;
We see by this, it was not sex;
     We see, we saw not, what did move:

But as all several souls contain
     Mixture of things they know not what,
Love these mix'd souls doth mix again,
     And makes both one, each this, and that.

A single violet transplant,
     The strength, the colour, and the size —
All which before was poor and scant —
     Redoubles still, and multiplies.

When love with one another so
      Interanimates two souls,
That abler soul, which thence doth flow,
      Defects of loneliness controls.

We then, who are this new soul, know,
      Of what we are composed, and made,
For th' atomies of which we grow
      Are souls, whom no change can invade.

But, O alas! so long, so far,
      Our bodies why do we forbear?
They are ours, though not we; we are
      Th' intelligences, they the spheres.

We owe them thanks, because they thus
      Did us, to us, at first convey,
Yielded their forces, sense, to us,
      Nor are dross to us, but allay.

On man heaven's influence works not so,
    But that it first imprints the air;
So soul into the soul may flow,
    Though it to body first repair.

As our blood labours to beget
    Spirits, as like souls as it can;
Because such fingers need to knit
    That subtle knot, which makes us man;

So must pure lovers' souls descend
    To affections, and to faculties,
Which sense may reach and apprehend,
    Else a great prince in prison lies.

To our bodies turn we then, that so
    Weak men on love reveal'd may look ;
Love's mysteries in souls do grow,
    But yet the body is his book.

And if some lover, such as we,
    Have heard this dialogue of one,
Let him still mark us, he shall see
    Small change when we're to bodies gone.

John Donne

To His Mistress Going To Bed

Come madam, come, all rest my powers defy;
Until I labour, I in labour lie.
The foe ofttimes, having the foe in sight,
Is tired with standing, though he never fight.
Off with that girdle, like heaven's zone glittering,
But a far fairer world encompassing.
Unpin that spangled breast-plate, which you wear,
That th' eyes of busy fools may be stopp'd there.
Unlace yourself, for that harmonious chime
Tells me from you that now it is bed-time.
Off with that happy busk, which I envy,
That still can be, and still can stand so nigh.
Your gown going off such beauteous state reveals,
As when from flowery meads th' hill's shadow steals.
Off with your wiry coronet, and show
The hairy diadem which on you doth grow.
Off with your hose and shoes; then softly tread
In this love's hallow'd temple, this soft bed.
In such white robes heaven's angels used to be
Revealed to men; thou, angel, bring'st with thee
A heaven-like Mahomet's paradise; and though
Ill spirits walk in white, we easily know
By this these angels from an evil sprite;
Those set our hairs, but these our flesh upright.

Licence my roving hands, and let them go
Before, behind, between, above, below.
O, my America, my Newfoundland,
My kingdom, safest when with one man mann'd,
My mine of precious stones, my empery;
How blest am I in this discovering thee!
To enter in these bonds, is to be free;
Then, where my hand is set, my seal shall be.
Full nakedness ! All joys are due to thee;
As souls unbodied, bodies unclothed must be
To taste whole joys. Gems which you women use
Are like Atlanta's ball cast in men's views;
That, when a fool's eye lighteth on a gem,
His earthly soul may covert theirs, not them:
Like pictures, or like books' gay coverings made
For laymen, are all women thus array'd.
Themselves are mystic books, which only we
— Whom their imputed grace will dignify —
Must see reveal'd. Then, since that I may know,
As liberally as to thy midwife show
Thyself; cast all, yea, this white linen hence;
There is no penance much less innocence:
To teach thee, I am naked first; why then,
What needst thou have more covering than a man?

John Donne

To Mary

I sleep with thee, and wake with thee,
And yet thou art not there;
I fill my arms with thoughts of thee,
And press the common air,
Thy eyes are gazing upon mine,
When thou art out of sight;
My lips are always touching thine,
At morning, noon, and night.

I think and speak of other things
To keep my mind at rest;
But still to thee my memory clings
Like love in woman's breast.
I hide it from the world's wide eye,
And think and speak contrary;
But soft the wind comes from the sky,
And whispers tales of Mary.

The night wind whispers in my ear,
The moon shines in my face;
A burden still of chilling fear
I find in every place.
The breeze is whispering in the bush,
And the dews fall from the tree,
All sighing on, and will not hush,
Some pleasant tales of thee.

John Clare

The Apparition

When by thy scorne, O murdresse, I am dead,
   And that thou thinkst thee free
From all solicitation from mee,
Then shall my ghost come to thy bed,
And thee, fain'd vestall, in worse armes shall see;
Then thy sicke taper will begin to winke,
And he, whose thou art then, being tyr'd before,
Will, if thou stirre, or pinch to wake him, thinke
   Thou call'st for more,
And in false sleepe will from thee shrinke,
And then poore Aspen wretch, neglected thou
Bath'd in a cold quicksilver sweat wilt lye
   A veryer ghost than I;
What I will say, I will not tell thee now,
Lest that preserve thee; and since my love is spent,
I'd rather thou shouldst painfully repent,
Than by my threatenings rest still innocent.

John Donne

Strange Fits of Passion Have I Known

Strange fits of passion have I known:
And I will dare to tell,
But in the Lover's ear alone,
What once to me befell.

When she I loved looked every day
Fresh as a rose in June,
I to her cottage bent my way,
Beneath an evening moon.

Upon the moon I fixed my eye,
All over the wide lea;
With quickening pace my horse drew nigh
Those paths so dear to me.

And now we reached the orchard-plot;
And, as we climbed the hill,
The sinking moon to Lucy's cot
Came near, and nearer still.

In one of those sweet dreams I slept,
Kind Nature's gentlest boon!
And all the while my eyes I kept
On the descending moon.

My horse moved on; hoof after hoof
He raised, and never stopped:
When down behind the cottage roof,
At once, the bright moon dropped.

What fond and wayward thoughts will slide
Into a Lover's head!
'O mercy!' to myself I cried,
'If Lucy should be dead!'

William Wordsworth

Longing

Come to me in my dreams, and then
By day I shall be well again!
For then the night will more than pay
The hopeless longing of the day.

Come, as thou cam'st a thousand times,
A messenger from radiant climes,
And smile on thy new world, and be
As kind to others as to me!

Or, as thou never cam'st in sooth,
Come now, and let me dream it truth,
And part my hair, and kiss my brow,
And say, My love! why sufferest thou?

Come to me in my dreams, and then
By day I shall be well again!
For then the night will more than pay
The hopeless longing of the day.

Matthew Arnold

Sudden Light

I have been here before,
　　But when or how I cannot tell:
I know the grass beyond the door,
　　The sweet keen smell,
The sighing sound, the lights around the shore.

You have been mine before, —
　　How long ago I may not know:
But just when at that swallow's soar
　　Your neck turned so,
Some veil did fall, — I knew it all of yore.

Has this been thus before?
　　And shall not thus time's eddying flight
Still with our lives our love restore
　　In death's despite,
And day and night yield one delight once more?

Dante Gabriel Rossetti

Love Is Enough

Love is enough: though the World be a-waning,
And the woods have no voice but the voice of complaining,
 Though the sky be too dark for dim eyes to discover
The gold-cups and daisies fair blooming thereunder,
Though the hills be held shadows, and the sea a dark wonder,
 And this day draw a veil over all deeds pass'd over,
Yet their hands shall not tremble, their feet shall not falter;
The void shall not weary, the fear shall not alter
 These lips and these eyes of the loved and the lover.

William Morris

Your Letter, Lady, Came Too Late

Your letter, lady, came too late,
    For Heaven had claimed its own.
Ah, sudden change — from prison rats
    Unto the great white throne!
And yet I think he would have stayed
    To live for his disdain,
Could he have read the careless words
    Which you have sent in vain.

So full of patience did he wait
    Through many a weary hour,
That o'er his simple soldier faith
    Not even death had power.
And you — did others whisper low
    Their homage in your ear,
As though among their shadowy throng
    His spirit had a peer.

I would that you were by me now,
    To draw the sheet aside,
And see how pure the look he wore
    The moment when he died.
The sorrow that you gave him
    Had left its weary trace,
As 'twere the shadow of the cross
    Upon his pallid face.

'Her love,' he said, 'could change for me
        The winter's cold to spring.'
Ah, trust of fickle maiden's love,
        Thou art a bitter thing!
For when these valleys bright in May
        Once more with blossoms wave,
The northern violets shall blow
        Above his humble grave.

Your dole of scanty words had been
        But one more pang to bear,
For him who kissed unto the last
        Your tress of golden hair.
I did not put it where he said,
        For when the angels come
I would not have them find the sign
        Of falsehood in the tomb.

I've seen your letter and I know
        The wiles that you have wrought
To win that noble heart of his,
        And gained it — cruel thought!
What lavish wealth men sometimes give
        For what is worthless all:
What manly bosoms beat for them
        In folly's falsest thrall.

You shall not pity him, for now
        His sorrow has an end,
Yet would that you could stand with me
        Beside my fallen friend.
And I forgive you for his sake
        As he — if it be given —
May even be pleading grace for you
        Before the court of Heaven.

Tonight the cold wind whistles by
        As I, my vigil keep
Within the prison dead house, where
        Few mourners come to weep.
A rude plank coffin holds his form,
        Yet death exalts his face
And I would rather see him thus
        Than clasped in your embrace.

Tonight your home may shine with lights
        And ring with merry song,
And you be smiling as your soul
        Had done no deadly wrong.
Your hand so fair that none would think
        It penned these words of pain;
Your skin so white — would God, your heart
        Were half as free from stain.

I'd rather be my comrade dead,
    Than you in life supreme:
For yours the sinner's waking dread,
    And his the martyr's dream.
Whom serve we in this life, we serve
    In that which is to come:
He chose his way, you yours; let God
    Pronounce the fitting doom.

W. S. Hawkins

To Lucasta, On Going To The Wars

Tell me not, Sweet, I am unkind,
    That from the nunnery
Of thy chaste breast, and quiet mind,
    To war and arms I fly.

True, a new mistress now I chase,
    The first foe in the field;
And with a stronger faith embrace
    A sword, a horse, a shield.

Yet this inconstancy is such,
    As you too shall adore;
I could not love thee, Dear, so much,
    Loved I not honour more.

Richard Lovelace

La Belle Dame Sans Merci

O what can ail thee, knight-at-arms,
    Alone and palely loitering?
The sedge has withered from the lake,
    And no birds sing.

O what can ail thee, knight-at-arms,
    So haggard and so woebegone?
The squirrel's granary is full,
    And the harvest's done.

I see a lily on thy brow
    With anguish moist and fever dew,
And on thy cheek a fading rose
    Fast withereth too.

I met a lady in the meads,
    Full beautiful — a faery's child,
Her hair was long, her foot was light,
    And her eyes were wild.

I made a garland for her head,
      And bracelets too, and fragrant zone;
She looked at me as she did love,
      And made sweet moan.

I set her on my pacing steed,
      And nothing else saw all day long,
For sidelong would she bend, and sing
      A faery's song.

She found me roots of relish sweet,
      And honey wild, and manna dew,
And sure in language strange she said
      'I love thee true.'

She took me to her elfin grot,
      And there she wept, and sighed full sore,
And there I shut her wild wild eyes
      With kisses four.

And there she lulled me asleep,
     And there I dreamed —Ah! woe betide!
The latest dream I ever dreamed
     On the cold hill's side.

I saw pale kings and princes too,
     Pale warriors, death-pale were they all;
They cried — '*La Belle Dame sans Merci*
     Hath thee in thrall!'

I saw their starved lips in the gloam,
     With horrid warning gaped wide,
And I awoke and found me here,
     On the cold hill's side.

And this is why I sojourn here,
     Alone and palely loitering,
Though the sedge has withered from the lake,
     And no birds sing.

John Keats

The Lady Of Shalott

On either side the river lie
Long fields of barley and of rye,
That clothe the wold and meet the sky;
And through the field the road run by
　　To many-tower'd Camelot;
And up and down the people go,
Gazing where the lilies blow
Round an island there below,
　　The island of Shalott.

Willows whiten, aspens quiver,
Little breezes dusk and shiver
Through the wave that runs for ever
By the island in the river
　　Flowing down to Camelot.
Four grey walls, and four grey towers,
Overlook a space of flowers,
And the silent isle imbowers
　　The Lady of Shalott.

By the margin, willow veil'd,
Slide the heavy barges trail'd
By slow horses; and unhail'd
The shallop flitteth silken-sail'd
　　Skimming down to Camelot:
But who hath seen her wave her hand?
Or at the casement seen her stand?
Or is she known in all the land,
　　The Lady of Shalott?

Only reapers, reaping early,
In among the bearded barley
Hear a song that echoes cheerly
From the river winding clearly;
    Down to tower'd Camelot;
And by the moon the reaper weary,
Piling sheaves in uplands airy,
Listening, whispers, 'Tis the fairy
    The Lady of Shalott.'

There she weaves by night and day
A magic web with colours gay.
She has heard a whisper say,
A curse is on her if she stay
    To look down to Camelot.
She knows not what the curse may be,
And so she weaveth steadily,
And little other care hath she,
    The Lady of Shalott.

And moving through a mirror clear
That hangs before her all the year,
Shadows of the world appear.
There she sees the highway near
    Winding down to Camelot;
There the river eddy whirls,
And there the surly village churls,
And the red cloaks of market girls
    Pass onward from Shalott.

Sometimes a troop of damsels glad,
An abbot on an ambling pad,
Sometimes a curly shepherd lad,
Or long-hair'd page in crimson clad
    Goes by to tower'd Camelot;
And sometimes through the mirror blue
The knights come riding two and two.
She hath no loyal Knight and true,
    The Lady of Shalott.

But in her web she still delights
To weave the mirror's magic sights,
For often through the silent nights
A funeral, with plumes and lights
    And music, went to Camelot;
Or when the Moon was overhead,
Came two young lovers lately wed.
'I am half sick of shadows,' said
    The Lady of Shalott.

A bow-shot from her bower-eaves,
He rode between the barley sheaves,
The sun came dazzling thro' the leaves,
And flamed upon the brazen greaves
    Of bold Sir Lancelot.
A red-cross knight for ever kneel'd
To a lady in his shield,
That sparkled on the yellow field,
    Beside remote Shalott.

The gemmy bridle glitter'd free,
Like to some branch of stars we see
Hung in the golden Galaxy.
The bridle bells rang merrily
  As he rode down to Camelot:
And from his blazon'd baldric slung
A mighty silver bugle hung,
And as he rode his armour rung
  Beside remote Shalott.

All in the blue unclouded weather
Thick-jewell'd shone the saddle-leather,
The helmet and the helmet-feather
Burn'd like one burning flame together,
  As he rode down to Camelot.
As often thro' the purple night,
Below the starry clusters bright,
Some bearded meteor, burning bright,
  Moves over still Shalott.

His broad clear brow in sunlight glow'd;
On burnish'd hooves his war-horse trode;
From underneath his helmet flow'd
His coal-black curls as on he rode,
  As he rode down to Camelot.
From the bank and from the river
He flashed into the crystal mirror,
'Tirra lirra,' by the river
  Sang Sir Lancelot.

She left the web, she left the loom,
She made three paces through the room,
She saw the water-lily bloom,
She saw the helmet and the plume,
        She look'd down to Camelot.
Out flew the web and floated wide;
The mirror crack'd from side to side;
'The curse is come upon me,' cried
        The Lady of Shalott.

In the stormy east-wind straining,
The pale yellow woods were waning,
The broad stream in his banks complaining.
Heavily the low sky raining
        Over tower'd Camelot;
Down she came and found a boat
Beneath a willow left afloat,
And around about the prow she wrote
        The Lady of Shalott.

And down the river's dim expanse
Like some bold seer in a trance,
Seeing all his own mischance —
With a glassy countenance
        Did she look to Camelot.
And at the closing of the day
She loosed the chain, and down she lay;
The broad stream bore her far away,
        The Lady of Shalott.

Lying, robed in snowy white
That loosely flew to left and right —
The leaves upon her falling light —
Thro' the noises of the night,
　　　She floated down to Camelot:
And as the boat-head wound along
The willowy hills and fields among,
They heard her singing her last song,
　　　The Lady of Shalott.

Heard a carol, mournful, holy,
Chanted loudly, chanted lowly,
Till her blood was frozen slowly,
And her eyes were darkened wholly,
　　　Turn'd to tower'd Camelot.
For ere she reach'd upon the tide
The first house by the water-side,
Singing in her song she died,
　　　The Lady of Shalott.

Under tower and balcony,
By garden-wall and gallery,
A gleaming shape she floated by,
Dead-pale between the houses high,
　　　Silent into Camelot.
Out upon the wharfs they came,
Knight and Burgher, Lord and Dame,
And around the prow they read her name,
　　　The Lady of Shalott.

Who is this? And what is here?
And in the lighted palace near
Died the sound of royal cheer;
And they crossed themselves for fear,
    All the Knights at Camelot;
But Lancelot mused a little space
He said, 'She has a lovely face;
God in his mercy lend her grace,
    The Lady of Shalott.'

Alfred, Lord Tennyson

Travel and Place

From A Railway Carriage

Faster than fairies, faster than witches,
Bridges and houses, hedges and ditches;
And charging along like troops in a battle
All through the meadows the horses and cattle:
All of the sights of the hill and the plain
Fly as thick as driving rain;
And ever again, in the wink of an eye,
Painted stations whistle by.

Here is a child who clambers and scrambles,
All by himself and gathering brambles;
Here is a tramp who stands and gazes;
And there is the green for stringing the daisies!
Here is a cart run away in the road
Lumping along with man and load;
And here is a mill, and there is a river:
Each a glimpse and gone for ever!

Robert Louis Stevenson

London

I wander through each chartered street,
Near where the chartered Thames does flow,
And mark in every face I meet,
Marks of weakness, marks of woe.

In every cry of every man,
In every infant's cry of fear,
In every voice, in every ban,
The mind-forged manacles I hear:

How the chimney-sweeper's cry
Every blackening church appalls,
And the hapless soldier's sigh
Runs in blood down palace walls.

But most, through midnight streets I hear
How the youthful harlot's curse
Blasts the new-born infant's tear,
And blights with plagues the marriage hearse.

William Blake

Composed Upon Westminster Bridge
Sept. 3, 1802

Earth has not anything to show more fair:
Dull would he be of soul who could pass by
A sight so touching in its majesty:
This City now doth like a garment wear
The beauty of the morning; silent, bare,
Ships, towers, domes, theatres, and temples lie
Open unto the fields, and to the sky;
All bright and glittering in the smokeless air.
Never did sun more beautifully steep
In his first splendour, valley, rock, or hill;
Ne'er saw I, never felt, a calm so deep!
The river glideth at his own sweet will:
Dear God! the very houses seem asleep;
And all that mighty heart is lying still!

William Wordsworth

Exile

I chose the place where I would rest
When death should come to claim me,
With the red-rose roots to wrap my breast
And a quiet stone to name me.

But I am laid on a northern steep
With the roaring tides below me,
And only the frosts to bind my sleep,
And only the winds to know me.

Marjorie Pickthall

Symphony In Yellow

An omnibus across the bridge
Crawls like a yellow butterfly,
And, here and there a passer-by
Shows like a little restless midge.

Big barges full of yellow hay
Are moored against the shadowy wharf,
And, like a yellow silken scarf,
The thick fog hangs along the quay.

The yellow leaves begin to fade
And flutter from the Temple elms,
And at my feet the pale green Thames
Lies like a rod of rippled jade.

Oscar Wilde

The Way Through The Woods

They shut the road through the woods
Seventy years ago.
Weather and rain have undone it again,
And now you would never know
There was once a road through the woods
Before they planted the trees.
It is underneath the coppice and heath,
And the thin anemones.
Only the keeper sees
That, where the ring-dove broods,
And the badgers roll at ease,
There was once a road through the woods.

Yet, if you enter the woods
Of a summer evening late,
When the night-air cools on the trout-ringed pools
Where the otter whistles his mate,
(They fear not men in the woods,
Because they see so few);
You will hear the beat of a horse's feet,
And the swish of a skirt in the dew,
Steadily cantering through
The misty solitudes,
As though they perfectly knew
The old lost road through the woods . . .
But there is no road through the woods.

Rudyard Kipling

Wenlock Edge

On Wenlock Edge the wood's in trouble;
    His forest fleece the Wrekin heaves;
The gale, it plies the saplings double,
    And thick on Severn snow the leaves.

'Twould blow like this through holt and hanger
    When Uricon the city stood;
'Tis the old wind in the old anger,
    But then it threshed another wood.

Then, 'twas before my time, the Roman
    At yonder heaving hill would stare:
The blood that warms an English yeoman,
    The thoughts that hurt him, they were there.

There, like the wind through woods in riot,
    Through him the gale of life blew high;
The tree of man was never quiet:
    Then 'twas the Roman, now 'tis I.

The gale, it plies the saplings double,
    It blows so hard, 'twill soon be gone:
Today the Roman and his trouble
    Are ashes under Uricon.

A. E. Housman

Dover Beach

The sea is calm to-night.
The tide is full, the moon lies fair
Upon the straits; on the French coast the light
Gleams and is gone; the cliffs of England stand;
Glimmering and vast, out in the tranquil bay.
Come to the window, sweet is the night-air!
Only, from the long line of spray
Where the sea meets the moon-blanched land,
Listen! you hear the grating roar
Of pebbles which the waves draw back, and fling,
At their return, up the high strand,
Begin, and cease, and then again begin,
With tremulous cadence slow, and bring
The eternal note of sadness in.

Sophocles long ago
Heard it in the Aegaean, and it brought
Into his mind the turbid ebb and flow
Of human misery; we
Find also in the sound a thought,
Hearing it by this distant northern sea.

The Sea of Faith
Was once, too, at the full, and round earth's shore
Lay like the folds of a bright girdle furled.
But now I only hear
Its melancholy, long, withdrawing roar,
Retreating, to the breath
Of the night-wind, down the vast edges drear
And naked shingles of the world.

Ah, love, let us be true
To one another! for the world, which seems
To lie before us like a land of dreams,
So various, so beautiful, so new,
Hath really neither joy, nor love, nor light,
Nor certitude, nor peace, nor help for pain;
And we are here as on a darkling plain
Swept with confused alarms of struggle and flight,
Where ignorant armies clash by night.

Matthew Arnold

Home Thoughts, From Abroad

Oh, to be in England
Now that April's there,
And whoever wakes in England
Sees, some morning, unaware,
That the lowest boughs and the brushwood sheaf
Round the elm-tree bole are in tiny leaf,
While the chaffinch sings on the orchard bough
In England — now!

And after April, when May follows,
And the whitethroat builds, and all the swallows!
Hark, where my blossom'd pear-tree in the hedge
Leans to the field and scatters on the clover
Blossoms and dewdrops — at the bent spray's edge —
That's the wise thrush; he sings each song twice over,
Lest you should think he never could recapture
The first fine careless rapture!
And though the fields look rough with hoary dew,
All will be gay when noontide wakes anew
The buttercups, the little children's dower
 — Far brighter than this gaudy melon-flower!

Robert Browning

My Heart's In The Highlands

My heart's in the Highlands, my heart is not here;
My heart's in the Highlands a-chasing the deer;
A-chasing the wild deer, and following the roe,
My heart's in the Highlands wherever I go.

Farewell to the Highlands, farewell to the North,
The birthplace of Valour, the country of Worth;
Wherever I wander, wherever I rove,
The hills of the Highlands for ever I love.

Farewell to the mountains high covered with snow;
Farewell to the straths and green valleys below;
Farewell to the forests and wild-hanging woods;
Farewell to the torrents and loud-pouring floods.

My heart's in the Highlands, my heart is not here;
My heart's in the Highlands a-chasing the deer;
A-chasing the wild deer, and following the roe,
My heart's in the Highlands wherever I go.

Robert Burns

A Niagara Landscape

Heavy with haze that merges and melts free
Into the measureless depth on either hand,
The full day rests upon the luminous land
In one long noon of golden reverie.
Now hath the harvest come and gone with glee.
The shaven fields stretch smooth and clean away,
Purple and green, and yellow, and soft grey,
Chequered with orchards. Farther still I see
Towns and dim villages, whose roof-tops fill
The distant mist, yet scarcely catch the view.
Thorold set sultry on its plateau'd hill,
And far to westward, where yon pointed towers
Rise faint and ruddy from the vaporous blue,
Saint Catharines, city of the host of flowers.

Archibald Lampman

A Canadian Boat Song

Faintly as tolls the evening chime
Our voices keep tune and our oars keep time.
Soon as the woods on shore look dim,
We'll sing at St. Anne's our parting hymn.
Row, brothers, row, the stream runs fast,
The rapids are near and the daylight's past.

Why should we yet our sail unfurl?
There is not a breath the blue wave to curl.
But when the wind blows off the shore,
Oh! sweetly we'll rest our weary oar.
Blow, breezes, blow, the stream runs fast,
The rapids are near and the daylight's past.

Utawas' tide! this trembling moon
Shall see us float over thy surges soon.
Saint of this green isle! hear our prayers,
Oh, grant us cool heavens and favouring airs.
Blow, breezes, blow, the stream runs fast,
The rapids are near and the daylight's past.

Thomas Moore

A Psalm Of Montreal

Stowed away in a Montreal lumber room
The Discobolus standeth and turneth his face to the wall;
Dusty, cobweb-covered, maimed and set at naught,
Beauty crieth in an attic and no man regardeth:
        O God! O Montreal!

Beautiful by night and day, beautiful in summer and winter,
Whole or maimed, always and alike beautiful
He preacheth gospel of grace to the skin of owls
And to one who seasoneth the skins of Canadian owls:
        O God! O Montreal!

When I saw him I was wroth and I said, 'O Discobolus!
Beautiful Discobolus, a Prince both among gods and men!
What doest thou here, how camest thou hither, Discobolus,
Preaching gospel in vain to the skins of owls?'
        O God! O Montreal!

And I turned to the man of skins and said unto him, 'O thou man
    of skins,
Wherefore hast thou done thus to shame the beauty of the
    Discobolus?'
But the Lord had hardened the heart of the man of skins
And he answered, 'My brother-in-law is haberdasher to
    Mr. Spurgeon.'
        O God! O Montreal!

'The Discobolus is put here because he is vulgar
He has neither vest nor pants with which to cover his limbs;
I, Sir, am a person of most respectable connections
My brother-in-law is haberdasher to Mr. Spurgeon.'
　　　　　O God! O Montreal!

Then I said, 'O brother-in-law to Mr. Spurgeon's haberdasher,
Who seasonest also the skins of Canadian owls,
Thou callest trousers "pants", whereas I call them "trousers"
Therefore thou art in hell-fire and may the Lord pity thee!'
　　　　　O God! O Montreal!

'Preferrest thou the gospel of Montreal to the gospel of Hellas,
The gospel of thy connection with Mr. Spurgeon's haberdashery
　　to the gospel of Discobolus?'
Yet none the less blasphemed he beauty saying, 'The Discobolus
　　hath no gospel,
But my brother-in-law is haberdasher to Mr. Spurgeon.'
　　　　　O God! O Montreal!

Samuel Butler

Home Thoughts, From The Sea

Nobly, nobly, Cape Saint Vincent to the Northwest died
away;
Sunset ran, one glorious blood-red, reeking into Cadiz
Bay;
Bluish 'mid the burning water, full in face Trafalgar lay;
In the dimmest Northeast distance dawned Gibraltar
grand and gray;
'Here and here did England help me: how can I help
England?' — say,
Whoso turns as I, this evening, turn to God to praise and
pray,
While Jove's planet rises yonder, silent over Africa.

Robert Browning

Adlestrop

Yes. I remember Adlestrop —
The name, because one afternoon
Of heat the express-train drew up there
Unwontedly. It was late June.

The steam hissed. Someone cleared his throat
No one left and no one came
On the bare platform. What I saw
Was Adlestrop — only the name

And willows, willow-herb, and grass,
And meadowsweet, and haycocks dry,
No whit less still and lonely fair
Than the high cloudlets in the sky.

And for that minute a blackbird sang
Close by, and round him, mistier,
Farther and farther, all the birds
Of Oxfordshire and Gloucestershire.

Edward Thomas

North Labrador

A land of leaning ice
Hugged by plaster-grey arches of sky,
Flings itself silently
Into eternity.

'Has no one come here to win you,
Or left you with the faintest blush
Upon your glittering breasts?
Have you no memories, O Darkly Bright?'

Cold-hushed, there is only the shifting of moments
That journey toward no Spring —
No birth, no death, no time nor sun
In answer.

Hart Crane

Midnight On The Great Western

In the third-class seat sat the journeying boy,
And the roof-lamp's oily flame
Played down on his listless form and face,
Bewrapt past knowing to what he was going,
Or whence he came.

In the band of his hat the journeying boy
Had a ticket stuck; and a string
Around his neck bore the key of his box,
That twinkled gleams of the lamp's sad beams
Like a living thing.

What past can be yours, O journeying boy
Towards a world unknown,
Who calmly, as if incurious quite
On all at stake, can undertake
This plunge alone?

Knows your soul a sphere, O journeying boy,
Our rude realms far above,
Whence with spacious vision you mark and mete
This region of sin that you find you in,
But are not of?

Thomas Hardy

On A Rhine Steamer

Republic of the West
    Enlightened, free, sublime,
Unquestionably best
    Production of our time,

The telephone is thine,
    And thine the Pullman car,
The caucus, the divine
    Intense electric star.

To thee we likewise owe
    The venerable names
Of Edgar Allan Poe,
    And Mr. Henry James.

In short it's due to thee,
    Thou kind of Western star,
That we have come to be
    Precisely what we are.

But every now and then,
    It cannot be denied,
You breed a kind of men
    Who are not dignified,

Or courteous or refined,
    Benevolent or wise,
Or gifted with a mind
    Beyond the common size,

Or notable for tact,
    Agreeable to me,
Or anything, in fact,
    That people ought to be.

J. K. Stephen

The Banks o' Doon

Ye flowery banks o' bonnie Doon,
How can ye blume sae fair!
How can ye chant, ye little birds,
And I sae fu' o' care!

Thou'll break my heart, thou bonnie bird,
That sings upon the bough;
Thou minds me o' the happy days
When my fause luve was true.

Thou'll break my heart, thou bonnie bird,
That sings beside thy mate;
For sae I sat, and sae I sang,
And wist na o' my fate.

Aft hae I roved by bonnie Doon,
To see the woodbine twine;
And ilka bird sang o' its luve,
And sae did I o' mine.

Wi' lightsome heart I pu'd a rose
Frae off its thorny tree;
And my fause luver staw the rose,
But left the thorn wi' me.

Robert Burns

Sweet Afton

Flow gently, sweet Afton, among thy green braes,
Flow gently, I'll sing thee a song in thy praise;
My Mary's asleep by the murmuring stream,
Flow gently, sweet Afton, disturb not her dream.

Thou stock-dove whose echo resounds thro' the glen,
Ye wild whistling blackbirds in yon thorny den,
Thou green-crested lapwing, thy screaming forbear,
I charge you, disturb not my slumbering fair.

How lofty, sweet Afton, thy neighbouring hills,
Far marked with the courses of clear, winding rills;
There daily I wander, as noon rises high,
My flocks and my Mary's sweet cot in my eye.

How pleasant thy banks and green valleys below,
Where wild in the woodlands the primroses blow;
There oft, as mild ev'ning weeps over the lea,
The sweet-scented birk shades my Mary and me.

Thy crystal stream, Afton, how lovely it glides,
And winds by the cot where my Mary resides;
How wanton thy waters her snowy feet lave,
As, gathering sweet flowerets, she stems thy clear wave.

Flow gently, sweet Afton, among thy green braes,
Flow gently, sweet river, the theme of my lays;
My Mary's asleep by thy murmuring stream,
Flow gently, sweet Afton, disturb not her dream.

Robert Burns

In Rotten Row

In Rotten Row a cigarette
I sat and smoked, with no regret
For all the tumult that had been.
The distances were still and green,
And streaked with shadows cool and wet.

Two sweethearts on a bench were set,
Two birds among the boughs were met;
So love and song were heard and seen
In Rotten Row.

A horse or two there was to fret
The soundless sand; but work and debt,
Fair flowers and falling leaves between,
While clocks are chiming clear and keen,
A man may very well forget
In Rotten Row.

William Ernest Henley

Facing West From California's Shores

Facing west, from California's shores,
Inquiring, tireless, seeking what is yet unfound,
I, a child, very old, over waves, towards the house of
     maternity, the land of migrations, look afar,
Look off the shores of my Western Sea — the circle
     almost circled;
For, starting westward from Hindustan, from the vales
     of Kashmere,
From Asia — from the north — from the God, the sage,
     and the hero,
From the south — from the flowery peninsulas, and the
     spice islands;
Long having wander'd since — round the earth having
     wander'd,
Now I face home again — very pleas'd and joyous;
(But where is what I started for, so long ago?
And why is it yet unfound?)

Walt Whitman

To Brooklyn Bridge

How many dawns, chill from his rippling rest
The seagull's wings shall dip and pivot him,
Shedding white rings of tumult, building high
Over the chained bay waters Liberty —

Then, with inviolate curve, forsake our eyes
As apparitional as sails that cross
Some page of figures to be filed away;
— Till elevators drop us from our day . . .

I think of cinemas, panoramic sleights
With multitudes bent toward some flashing scene
Never disclosed, but hastened to again,
Foretold to other eyes on the same screen;

And Thee, across the harbor, silver-paced
As though the sun took step of thee, yet left
Some motion ever unspent in thy stride, —
Implicitly thy freedom staying thee!

Out of some subway scuttle, cell or loft
A bedlamite speeds to thy parapets,
Tilting there momently, shrill shirt ballooning,
A jest falls from the speechless caravan.

Down Wall, from girder into street noon leaks,
A rip-tooth of the sky's acetylene;
All afternoon the cloud-flown derricks turn . . .
Thy cables breathe the North Atlantic still.

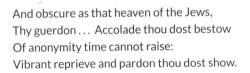

And obscure as that heaven of the Jews,
Thy guerdon ... Accolade thou dost bestow
Of anonymity time cannot raise:
Vibrant reprieve and pardon thou dost show.

O harp and altar, of the fury fused,
(How could mere toil align thy choiring strings!)
Terrific threshold of the prophet's pledge,
Prayer of pariah, and the lover's cry, —

Again the traffic lights that skim thy swift
Unfractioned idiom, immaculate sigh of stars,
Beading thy path — condense eternity:
And we have seen night lifted in thine arms.

Under thy shadow by the piers I waited;
Only in darkness is thy shadow clear.
The City's fiery parcels all undone,
Already snow submerges an iron year ...

O Sleepless as the river under thee,
Vaulting the sea, the prairies' dreaming sod,
Unto us lowliest sometime sweep, descend
And of the curveship lend a myth to God.

Hart Crane

Once I Pass'd Through A Populous City

Once I pass'd through a populous city imprinting my
brain for future use with its shows, architecture,
customs,
traditions,
Yet now of all that city I remember only a woman I
casually met there who detain'd me for love of me,
Day by day and night by night we were together — all
else has long been forgotten by me,
I remember I say only that woman who passionately clung
to me
Again we wander, we love, we separate again,
Again she holds me by the hand, I must not go,
I see her close beside me with silent lips sad and
tremulous.

Walt Whitman

I Travelled Among Unknown Men

I travelled among unknown men,
In lands beyond the sea;
Nor, England! did I know till then
What love I bore to thee.

'Tis past, that melancholy dream!
Nor will I quit thy shore
A second time; for still I seem
To love thee more and more.

Among thy mountains did I feel
The joy of my desire;
And she I cherished turned her wheel
Beside an English fire.

Thy mornings showed, thy nights concealed,
The bowers where Lucy played;
And thine too is the last green field
That Lucy's eyes surveyed.

William Wordsworth

I Knew By The Smoke That So Gracefully Curled

I knew by the smoke that so gracefully curled
    Above the green elms, that a cottage was near,
And I said, 'If there's peace to be found in the world,
    A heart that is humble might hope for it here!'

It was noon, and on flowers that languished around
    In silence reposed the voluptuous bee;
Every leaf was at rest, and I heard not a sound
    But the woodpecker tapping the hollow beech tree.

And 'Here in this lone little wood,' I exclaimed,
'   With a maid who was lovely to soul and to eye,
Who would blush when I praised her, and weep if
      I blamed,
How blest could I live, and how calm could I die!

'By the shade of yon sumach, whose red beity dips
    In the gush of the fountain, how sweet to recline,
And to know that I sighed upon innocent lips,
    Which had never been sighed on by any but mine!'

Thomas Moore

The Song Of Sheffield

Shells, shells, shells!
The song of the city of steel;
Hammer and turn, and file,
Furnace, and lathe, and wheel.
Tireless machinery,
Man's ingenuity,
Making a way for the martial devil's meal.

Shells, shells, shells!
Out of the furnace blaze;
Roll, roll, roll,
Into the workshop's maze.
Ruthless machinery
Boring eternally,
Boring a hole for the shattering charge that stays.

Shells, shells, shells!
The song of the city of steel;
List to the devils' mirth,
Hark to their laughters' peal:
Sheffield's machinery
Crushing humanity
Neath devil-ridden death's impassive heel.

Harold Beckh

Returning, We Hear the Larks

Sombre the night is.
And though we have our lives, we know
What sinister threat lies there.

Dragging these anguished limbs, we only know
This poison-blasted track opens on our camp—
On a little safe sleep.

But hark! joy — joy — strange joy.
Lo! heights of night ringing with unseen larks.
Music showering our upturned list'ning faces.

Death could drop from the dark
As easily as song—
But song only dropped,
Like a blind man's dreams on the sand
By dangerous tides,
Like a girl's dark hair for she dreams no ruin lies there,
Or her kisses where a serpent hides.

Isaac Rosenberg

Humour and Nonsense

Jabberwocky

'Twas brillig, and the slithy toves
Did gyre and gimble in the wabe;
All mimsy were the borogoves,
And the mome raths outgrabe.

'Beware the Jabberwock, my son!
The jaws that bite, the claws that catch!
Beware the Jubjub bird, and shun
The frumious Bandersnatch!'

He took his vorpal sword in hand:
Long time the manxome foe he sought —
So rested he by the Tumtum tree,
And stood awhile in thought.

And as in uffish thought he stood,
The Jabberwock, with eyes of flame,
Came whiffling through the tulgey wood,
And burbled as it came!

One, two! One, two! And through and through
The vorpal blade went snicker-snack!
He left it dead, and with its head
He went galumphing back.

'And hast thou slain the Jabberwock?
Come to my arms, my beamish boy!
O frabjous day! Callooh! Callay!'
He chortled in his joy.

'Twas brillig, and the slithy toves
Did gyre and gimble in the wabe;
All mimsy were the borogoves,
And the mome raths outgrabe.

Lewis Carroll

A Sonnet

O lovely O most charming pug
Thy gracefull air and heavenly mug
The beauties of his mind do shine
And every bit is shaped so fine
Your very tail is most devine
Your teeth is whiter than the snow
You are a great buck and a bow
Your eyes are of so fine a shape
More like a christains then an ape
His cheeks is like the roses blume
Your hair is like the raven's plume
His noses cast is of the roman
He is a very pretty weomen
I could not get a rhyme for roman
And was oblidged to call it weoman.

Marjory Fleming

The Walrus And The Carpenter

The sun was shining on the sea,
Shining with all his might:
He did his very best to make
The billows smooth and bright —
And this was odd, because it was
The middle of the night.

The moon was shining sulkily,
Because she thought the sun
Had got no business to be there
After the day was done —
'It's very rude of him,' she said,
'To come and spoil the fun.'

The sea was wet as wet could be,
The sands were dry as dry.
You could not see a cloud, because
No cloud was in the sky:
No birds were flying overhead —
There were no birds to fly.

The Walrus and the Carpenter
Were walking close at hand;
They wept like anything to see
Such quantities of sand:
'If this were only cleared away,'
They said, 'it would be grand.'

'If seven maids with seven mops
Swept it for half a year,
Do you suppose,' the Walrus said,
'That they could get it clear?'
'I doubt it,' said the Carpenter,
And shed a bitter tear.

'O Oysters, come and walk with us!'
The Walrus did beseech.
'A pleasant walk, a pleasant talk,
Along the briny beach:
We cannot do with more than four,
To give a hand to each.'

The eldest Oyster looked at him,
But never a word he said:
The eldest Oyster winked his eye,
And shook his heavy head —
Meaning to say he did not choose
To leave the oyster-bed.

But four young Oysters hurried up,
All eager for the treat:
Their coats were brushed, their faces washed,
Their shoes were clean and neat —
And this was odd, because, you know,
They hadn't any feet.

Four other Oysters followed them,
And yet another four;
And thick and fast they came at last,
And more, and more, and more —
All hopping through the frothy waves,
And scrambling to the shore.

The Walrus and the Carpenter
Walked on a mile or so,
And then they rested on a rock
Conveniently low:
And all the little Oysters stood
And waited in a row.

'The time has come,' the Walrus said,
'To talk of many things:
Of shoes — and ships — and sealing-wax —
Of cabbages — and kings —
And why the sea is boiling hot —
And whether pigs have wings.'

'But wait a bit,' the Oysters cried,
'Before we have our chat;
For some of us are out of breath,
And all of us are fat!'
'No hurry!' said the Carpenter.
They thanked him much for that.

'A loaf of bread,' the Walrus said,
'Is what we chiefly need:
Pepper and vinegar besides
Are very good indeed —
Now if you're ready, Oysters dear,
We can begin to feed.'

'But not on us!' the Oysters cried,
Turning a little blue.
'After such kindness, that would be
A dismal thing to do!'
'The night is fine,' the Walrus said,
'Do you admire the view?

'It was so kind of you to come!
And you are very nice!'
The Carpenter said nothing but
'Cut us another slice:
I wish you were not quite so deaf —
I've had to ask you twice!'

'It seems a shame,' the Walrus said,
'To play them such a trick,
After we've brought them out so far,
And made them trot so quick!'
The Carpenter said nothing but
'The butter's spread too thick!'

'I weep for you,' the Walrus said:
'I deeply sympathise.'
With sobs and tears he sorted out
Those of the largest size,
Holding his pocket-handkerchief
Before his streaming eyes.

'O Oysters,' said the Carpenter,
'You've had a pleasant run!
Shall we be trotting home again?'
But answer came there none —
And this was scarcely odd, because
They'd eaten every one.

Lewis Carroll

The Pig

It was an evening in November,
As I very well remember.
I was walking down the street in drunken pride,
And my knees were all a-flutter,
So I landed in the gutter,
And a pig walked up and laid down at my side.
Yes, I lay there in the gutter,
Thinking thoughts I could not utter,
When a colleen passing by did softly say,
'You can tell the man that boozes
By the company he chooses...'
At that, the pig got up and walked away.

Anonymous

A Terrible Infant

I recollect a nurse call'd Ann,
Who carried me about the grass,
And one fine day a fine young man
Came up, and kiss'd the pretty lass.
She did not make the least objection.
Thinks I, 'Aha!
When I can talk I'll tell Mama'
— And that's my earliest recollection.

Frederick Locker-Lampson

The Owl And The Pussy-Cat

The Owl and the Pussy-cat went to sea
    In a beautiful pea-green boat,
They took some honey, and plenty of money,
    Wrapped up in a five-pound note.
The Owl looked up to the stars above,
    And sang to a small guitar,
'O lovely Pussy! O Pussy, my love,
    What a beautiful Pussy you are,
        You are,
        You are!
What a beautiful Pussy you are!'

II

Pussy said to the Owl, 'You elegant fowl!
    How charmingly sweet you sing!
O let us be married! too long we have tarried:
    But what shall we do for a ring?'
They sailed away, for a year and a day,
    To the land where the Bong-tree grows
And there in a wood a Piggy-wig stood
    With a ring at the end of his nose,
        His nose,
        His nose,
With a ring at the end of his nose.

III
'Dear Pig, are you willing to sell for one shilling
    Your ring?' Said the Piggy, 'I will.'
So they took it away, and were married next day
    By the Turkey who lives on the hill.
They dined on mince, and slices of quince,
    Which they ate with a runcible spoon;
And hand in hand, on the edge of the sand,
    They danced by the light of the moon,
        The moon,
        The moon,
They danced by the light of the moon.

Edward Lear

How Pleasant To Know Mr Lear

'How pleasant to know Mr Lear!'
    Who has written such volumes of stuff!
Some think him ill-tempered and queer,
    But a few think him pleasant enough.

His mind is concrete and fastidious,
    His nose is remarkably big;
His visage is more or less hideous,
    His beard it resembles a wig.

He has ears, and two eyes, and ten fingers,
    Leastways if you reckon two thumbs;
Long ago he was one of the singers,
    But now he is one of the dumbs.

He sits in a beautiful parlour,
    With hundreds of books on the wall;
He drinks a great deal of Marsala,
    But never gets tipsy at all.

He has many friends, lay-men and clerical,
    Old Foss is the name of his cat;
His body is perfectly spherical,
    He weareth a runcible hat.

When he walks in waterproof white,
    The children run after him so!
Calling out, 'He's come out in his night-
    gown, that crazy old Englishman, oh!'

He weeps by the side of the ocean,
    He weeps on the top of the hill;
He purchases pancakes and lotion,
    And chocolate shrimps from the mill.

He reads, but he cannot speak, Spanish,
    He cannot abide ginger beer:
Ere the days of his pilgrimage vanish,
    How pleasant to know Mr Lear!

Edward Lear

Fable

The mountain and the squirrel
Had a quarrel;
And the former called the latter 'Little Prig';
Bun replied,
'You are doubtless very big;
But all sorts of things and weather
Must be taken in together
To make up a year
And a sphere.
And I think it no disgrace
To occupy my place.
If I'm not so large as you,
You are not so small as I,
And not half so spry.
I'll not deny you make
A very pretty squirrel track;
Talents differ: all is well and wisely put;
If I cannot carry forests on my back,
Neither can you crack a nut.'

Ralph Waldo Emerson

The Elephant, Or The Force of Habit

A tail behind, a trunk in front,
Complete the usual elephant.
The tail in front, the trunk behind
Is what you very seldom find.

If you for specimens should hunt
With trunks behind and tails in front,
That hunt would occupy you long;
The force of habit is so strong.

A. E. Housman

When Lovely Woman

When lovely woman wants a favor,
And finds, too late, that man won't bend,
What earthly circumstance can save her
From disappointment in the end?

The only way to bring him over,
The last experiment to try,
Whether a husband or a lover,
If he have feeling, is, to cry!

Phoebe Cary

Thy Heart

Thy heart is like some icy lake,
On whose cold brink I stand;
Oh, buckle on my spirit's skate,
And lead, thou living saint, the way
To where the ice is thin —
That it may break beneath my feet
And let a lover in!

Anonymous

Miniver Cheevy

Miniver Cheevy, child of scorn,
    Grew lean while he assailed the seasons;
He wept that he was ever born,
    And he had reasons.

Miniver loved the days of old
    When swords were bright and steeds were prancing;
The vision of a warrior bold
    Would send him dancing.

Miniver sighed for what was not,
    And dreamed, and rested from his labors;
He dreamed of Thebes and Camelot,
    And Priam's neighbors.

Miniver mourned the ripe renown
    That made so many a name so fragrant;
He mourned Romance, now on the town,
    And Art, a vagrant.

Miniver loved the Medici,
    Albeit he had never seen one;
He would have sinned incessantly
    Could he have been one.

Miniver cursed the commonplace
    And eyed a khaki suit with loathing:
He missed the medieval grace
    Of iron clothing.

Miniver scorned the gold he sought,
    But sore annoyed was he without it;
Miniver thought, and thought, and thought,
    And thought about it.

Miniver Cheevy, born too late,
    Scratched his head and kept on thinking;
Miniver coughed, and called it fate,
    And kept on drinking.

Edwin Arlington Robinson

The Pessimist

Nothing to do but work,
Nothing to eat but food,
Nothing to wear but clothes,
To keep one from going nude.

Nothing to breathe but air,
Quick as a flash 'tis gone;
Nowhere to fall but off,
Nowhere to stand but on.

Nothing to comb but hair,
Nowhere to sleep but in bed,
Nothing to weep but tears,
Nothing to bury but dead.

Nothing to sing but songs,
Ah, well, alas! alack!
Nowhere to go but out,
Nowhere to come but back.

Nothing to see but sights,
Nothing to quench but thirst,
Nothing to have but what we've got,
Thus through life we are cursed.

Nothing to strike but a gait;
Everything moves that goes.
Nothing at all but common sense
Can ever withstand these woes.

Ben King

Excelsior

The shades of night were falling fast
And the rain was falling faster,
When through an Alpine village passed
An Alpine village pastor;
A youth who bore mid snow and ice
A bird that wouldn't chirrup,
And a banner, with the strange device —
'Mrs. Winslow's soothing syrup.

'Beware the pass,' the old man said,
'My bold and desperate fellah;
Dark lowers the tempest overhead,
And you'll want your umberella;
And the roaring torrent is deep and wide —
You may hear how it washes.'
But still that clarion voice replied:
'I've got my old goloshes.'

'Oh stay,' the maiden said, 'and rest
(For the wind blows from the nor'ward)
Thy weary head upon my breast —
And please don't think me forward.'
A tear stood in his bright blue eye
And gladly he would have tarried;
But still he answered with a sigh:
'Unhappily I'm married.'

A. E. Housman

Ode On The Death Of A Favourite Cat, Drowned In A Tub Of Gold Fishes

'Twas on a lofty vase's side,
Where China's gayest art had dyed
The azure flowers that blow,
Demurest of the tabby kind,
The pensive Selima, reclined,
Gazed on the lake below.

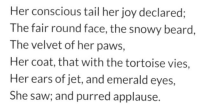

Her conscious tail her joy declared;
The fair round face, the snowy beard,
The velvet of her paws,
Her coat, that with the tortoise vies,
Her ears of jet, and emerald eyes,
She saw; and purred applause.

Still had she gazed; but 'midst the tide
Two angel forms were seen to glide,
The genii of the stream:
Their scaly armour's Tyrian hue
Through richest purple to the view
Betrayed a golden gleam.

The hapless nymph with wonder saw:
A whisker first, and then a claw,
With many an ardent wish,
She stretched, in vain, to reach the prize.
What female heart can gold despise?
What cat's averse to fish?

Presumptuous maid! with looks intent
Again she stretched, again she bent,
Nor knew the gulf between:
(Malignant Fate sat by, and smiled)
The slippery verge her feet beguiled,
She tumbled headlong in.

Eight times emerging from the flood
She mewed to ev''y wat'ry god
Some speedy aid to send.
No dolphin came, no nereid stirred;
Nor cruel Tom, nor Susan heard.
A fav'rite has no friend!

From hence, ye beauties undeceived,
Know, one false step is ne'er retrieved,
And be with caution bold.
Not all that tempts your wand'ring eyes
And heedless hearts is lawful prize;
Nor all that glisters, gold.

Thomas Gray

Elegy On The Death Of A Mad Dog

Good people all, of every sort,
Give ear unto my song;
And if you find it wond'rous short,
It cannot hold you long.

In Islington there was a man,
Of whom the world might say,
That still a godly race he ran,
Whene'er he went to pray.

A kind and gentle heart he had,
To comfort friends and foes;
The naked every day he clad,
When he put on his clothes.

And in that town a dog was found,
As many dogs there be,
Both mongrel, puppy, whelp and hound,
And curs of low degree.

This dog and man at first were friends;
But when a pique began,
The dog, to gain some private ends,
Went mad and bit the man.

Around from all the neighbouring streets
The wond'ring neighbours ran,
And swore the dog had lost its wits,
To bite so good a man.

The wound it seemed both sore and sad
To every Christian eye;
And while they swore the dog was mad,
They swore the man would die.

But soon a wonder came to light,
That showed the rogues they lied:
The man recovered of the bite,
The dog it was that died.

Oliver Goldsmith

Phyllis's Age

How old may Phyllis be, you ask,
Whose beauty thus all hearts engages?
To answer is no easy task;
For she has really two ages.

Stiff in brocard, and pinch'd in stays,
Her patches, paint, and jewels on;
All day let envy view her face;
And Phyllis is but twenty-one.

Paint, patches, jewels laid aside,
At night astronomers agree,
The evening has the day belied;
And Phyllis is some forty-three.

Matthew Prior

Jenny Kiss'd Me

Jenny kiss'd me when we met,
    Jumping from the chair she sat in;
Time, you thief, who love to get
    Sweets into your list, put that in!
Say I'm weary, say I'm sad,
    Say that health and wealth have miss'd me,
Say I'm growing old, but add —
    Jenny kiss'd me!

Leigh Hunt

How Doth The Little Crocodile

How doth the little crocodile
Improve his shining tail,
And pour the waters of the Nile
On every golden scale!

How cheerfully he seems to grin
How neatly spreads his claws,
And welcomes little fishes in,
With gently smiling jaws!

Lewis Carroll

The Jumblies

They went to sea in a Sieve, they did,
    In a Sieve they went to sea:
In spite of all their friends could say,
    On a winter's morn, on a stormy day,
In a Sieve they went to sea!
    And when the Sieve turned round and round,
And every one cried, 'You'll all be drowned!'
    They called aloud, 'Our Sieve ain't big,
But we don't care a button! we don't care a fig!
    In a Sieve we'll go to sea!'
      Far and few, far and few,
        Are the lands where the Jumblies live;
        Their heads are green, and their hands are blue,
            And they went to sea in a Sieve.

They sailed away in a Sieve, they did,
    In a Sieve they sailed so fast,
With only a beautiful pea-green veil
    Tied with a riband by way of a sail,
To a small tobacco-pipe mast;
    And every one said, who saw them go,
'O won't they be soon upset, you know!
    For the sky is dark, and the voyage is long,
And happen what may, it's extremely wrong
    In a Sieve to sail so fast!'
      Far and few, far and few,
        Are the lands where the Jumblies live;
        Their heads are green, and their hands are blue,
            And they went to sea in a Sieve.

The water it soon came in, it did,
    The water it soon came in;
So to keep them dry, they wrapped their feet
    In a pinky paper all folded neat,
And they fastened it down with a pin.
    And they passed the night in a crockery-jar,
And each of them said, 'How wise we are!
    Though the sky be dark, and the voyage be long,
Yet we never can think we were rash or wrong,
    While round in our Sieve we spin!'
        Far and few, far and few,
            Are the lands where the Jumblies live;
        Their heads are green, and their hands are blue,
                And they went to sea in a Sieve.

And all night long they sailed away;
    And when the sun went down,
They whistled and warbled a moony song
    To the echoing sound of a coppery gong,
In the shade of the mountains brown.
    'O Timballo! How happy we are,
When we live in a Sieve and a crockery-jar,
    And all night long in the moonlight pale,
We sail away with a pea-green sail,
    In the shade of the mountains brown!'
        Far and few, far and few,
            Are the lands where the Jumblies live;
        Their heads are green, and their hands are blue,
                And they went to sea in a Sieve.

They sailed to the Western Sea, they did,
    To a land all covered with trees,
And they bought an Owl, and a useful Cart,
    And a pound of Rice, and a Cranberry Tart,
And a hive of silvery Bees.
    And they bought a Pig, and some green Jack-daws,
And a lovely Monkey with lollipop paws,
    And forty bottles of Ring-Bo-Ree,
And no end of Stilton Cheese.
        Far and few, far and few,
            Are the lands where the Jumblies live;
        Their heads are green, and their hands are blue,
                And they went to sea in a Sieve.

And in twenty years they all came back,
    In twenty years or more,
And every one said, 'How tall they've grown!
    For they've been to the Lakes, and the Torrible Zone,
And the hills of the Chankly Bore!'
    And they drank their health, and gave them a feast
Of dumplings made of beautiful yeast;
    And every one said, 'If we only live,
We too will go to sea in a Sieve, —
    To the hills of the Chankly Bore!'
        Far and few, far and few,
            Are the lands where the Jumblies live;
        Their heads are green, and their hands are blue,
                And they went to sea in a Sieve.

Edward Lear

Wynken, Blynken, And Nod

Wynken, Blynken, and Nod one night
     Sailed off in a wooden shoe —
Sailed on a river of crystal light,
     Into a sea of dew.
'Where are you going, and what do you wish?'
     The old moon asked the three.
'We have come to fish for the herring fish
     That live in this beautiful sea;
Nets of silver and gold have we!'
        Said Wynken,
        Blynken,
        And Nod.

The old moon laughed and sang a song,
     As they rocked in the wooden shoe,
And the wind that sped them all night long
     Ruffled the waves of dew.
The little stars were the herring fish
     That lived in that beautiful sea —
'Now cast your nets wherever you wish —
Never afeard are we';
     So cried the stars to the fishermen three:
        Wynken,
        Blynken,
        And Nod.

All night long their nets they threw
    To the stars in the twinkling foam —
Then down from the skies came the wooden shoe,
    Bringing the fishermen home;
'Twas all so pretty a sail it seemed
    As if it could not be,
And some folks thought 'twas a dream they'd dreamed
    Of sailing that beautiful sea —
    But I shall name you the fishermen three:
        Wynken,
        Blynken,
        And Nod.

Wynken and Blynken are two little eyes,
    And Nod is a little head,
And the wooden shoe that sailed the skies
    Is a wee one's trundle-bed.
So shut your eyes while Mother sings
    Of wonderful sights that be,
And you shall see the beautiful things
    As you rock on the misty sea,
    Where the old shoe rocked the fishermen three:
        Wynken,
        Blynken,
        And Nod.

Eugene Field

Old Nick In Sorel

Old Nick took a fancy, as many men tell,
To come for a winter to live in Sorel.
Yet the snow fell so deep as he came in his sleigh,
That his fingers and toes were frost-nipt on the way.

In truth, said the demon, who'd ever suppose,
I must go back again with the loss of all those;
In either extreme, sure it matters me not,
If I freeze upon earth or at home I'm too hot;

So he put back his sleigh, for he thought it amiss,
His clime to compare to a climate like this;
And now 'tis resolved that this frightful new-comer
Will winter in hell and be here in the summer.

Standish O'Grady

The Boy Of Quebec

There was a young boy of Quebec
Who fell into the ice to his neck.
When asked, 'Are you friz?'
He replied, 'Yes, I is,
But we don't call this cold in Quebec.'

Rudyard Kipling

The Camel's Hump

The Camel's hump is an ugly lump
Which well you may see at the Zoo;
But uglier yet is the hump we get
From having too little to do.

Kiddies and grown-ups too-oo-oo,
If we haven't enough to do-oo-oo,
We get the hump —
Cameelious hump —
The hump that is black and blue!

We climb out of bed with a frouzly head,
And a snarly-yarly voice.
We shiver and scowl and we grunt and we growl
At our bath and our boots and our toys;

And there ought to be a corner for me
(And I know there is one for you)
When we get the hump —
Cameelious hump —
The hump that is black and blue!

The cure for this ill is not to sit still,
Or frowst with a book by the fire;
But to take a large hoe and a shovel also,
And dig till you gently perspire;

And then you will find that the sun and the wind,
And the Djinn of the Garden too,
Have lifted the hump —
The horrible hump —
The hump that is black and blue!

I get it as well as you-oo-oo,
If I haven't enough to do-oo-oo!
We all get hump —
Cameelious hump —
Kiddies and grown-ups too!

Rudyard Kipling

The Lazy Writer

In summer I'm disposed to shirk,
As summer is no time to work.
In winter inspiration dies
For lack of out-door exercise.
In spring I'm seldom in the mood,
Because of vernal lassitude.
The fall remains. But such a fall!
We've really had no fall at all.

Bert Leston Taylor

Index of Poets

Index of First Lines